A Personal Guide Into Happiness

PAT CLARKE

*Simple Steps To Inner Peace: A Personal Guide Into Happiness*
Copyright © 2022 by Pat Clarke. All rights reserved.

No part of this book may be used or reproduced in any manner whatsoever without written permission, except in the case of brief quotations embodied in critical articles and reviews. For more information, e-mail all inquiries to info@mindstirmedia.com.

The information offered in this book should not be taken as a substitute for professional medical treatment or psychological help. Following the steps in the book is at the reader's discretion and risk. The author cannot be held responsible for any loss, claim or damage arising out of the use, or misuse of the suggestions made.

Printed in the United States of America

ISBN: 978-1-80443-005-7 (Paperback)
ISBN: 978-1-80443-004-0 (eBook)

To Naomi

With big thanks for all your support while I'm not managing to put all this into practice!

Pat C ☺

# DEDICATION

For all who realise that peace in our world begins with peace in each human heart.

# CONTENTS

# WELCOME

Hello Dear Reader

Welcome to the start of this journey and congratulations for deciding to investigate the possibility of finding inner peace. When we are truly peaceful in our core, we can feel happy being who we are whatever happens around and to us. This not only feels good but enables us, through clarity and calmness, to respond in a helpful way for the benefit of ourselves and others. Becoming a more peaceful and therefore happier person not only has the obvious advantages for the one involved but can also lift the spirit of those around, and even help humanity as a whole. Each journey begins with a single step, followed by another and another and, when you think about it, all great explorations and adventures start in just this way. Some have a clear goal or destination, which may or may not be reached, while others are ventures into the unknown, sometimes inspired by an inner prompting that is not initially obvious. The steps I offer here can fit either of these categories, but I make this offering from the heart in order to share the route my inner journey has followed.

## *SIMPLE* STEPS?

In no way would I want to imply that it's simple to move out of depression, grief, deep despair, or to recover easily from current, recent, or past trauma. All deep emotion needs to be felt in order to be healed, and it takes time, courage and sometimes professional help to get through the process. We each have our own history of experiences of pain and joy that have impacted our lives and formed who we are today, and no one story can be judged better or worse, easier, or more difficult, than another. When we feel pain—physical, mental or emotional—only we know and suffer the depth of that and whether we have the will and the strength to deal with and grow out of it is up to the individual.

However, whether we choose to deal with these big issues or not, we still have everyday life to cope with, and I have found that having access to a special place within me can smooth the way through the ups and down of this daily journey. My hope is that the following processes will help you move away from everyday stresses and bring you more peace and a deeper sense of contentment by guiding you into that calm centre within. At first we notice the thoughts and reactions that are disturbing us and then learn to use practices that, over time, bring us more and more tranquillity. Even if you are currently in a dark place in your life, the methods here should provide some rays of light to at least smooth the ruffles of daily life while you work on the big stuff.

## AND WHO AM I?

You may naturally be wondering who I am to be offering you suggestions that could make a big difference to your life and why I am bothering to put this book together at all instead of just getting on with my happy retirement. Well, I would describe myself as **an ordinary person**—not an expert in anything in particular. I've had no great epiphanies or visions; have no special powers and I didn't grow up seeing fairies or hearing channelled voices. I've not been drawn into any particular religion, preferring to shape my own belief system from what feels true for me—and what works in my life. I've known huge lasting joy and periods of deep despair. I've felt blissfully loved and blessed a lot of the time but have also experienced feeling rejected, abandoned, smothered and even suicidal.

What I have found fascinating are the workings of our minds and emotions and, more latterly, how they connect with and affect our bodies in such an important and impactful way. I love learning and have come to realise that we can learn so much from ourselves by becoming aware of and listening to these three parts of us—mind, body, and emotions—our three allies who can help us achieve peace in our lives. In fact, I have come to discover that we actually have a place of deep peace within each of us and that, with practice, it is perfectly possible to access this whenever we wish and, indeed, to live within it all the time. This has recently led to a wish to share my findings with others in small practical groups and now in this handbook.

My journey started at a low point in my life, about 30 years ago, when, feeling very alone, I was made aware of the importance of noticing my emotions, and realised that I tended to try to avoid or override the negative ones, of which there were many at that time. A friend suggested it would be more helpful and healing to let myself notice and truly feel these feelings. It also made me realise how I had been travelling through my life up until then without much thought about what makes us tick, our differences, and how we could create the life we wanted. This was the start of my deep interest in the purpose, origin, and healing potential of all the emotions we humans experience on a daily basis, and also ignited an interest in psychology, healing, spirituality and many other aspects of self-discovery and development. Not only did I make discoveries about these things at a general, academic level, but I began to find ways of using this knowledge to learn more about myself, which led to me devising techniques and strategies for recognising and correcting the thoughts and behaviours that caused me stress, discomfort and even some physical problems. At that point I was indeed a beginner and just starting out on a very circuitous route to creating a calmer life.

## THE GUIDE

The techniques I offer here are sifted out and adapted from all the books, workshops, classes, discussions, and practices across those years, down to what I consider to be the main components of my process. This step-by-step guide walks you through the route I took to reach tranquillity, with the aim of getting you there more quickly. It is, of course, just one route among many.

Whether or not you are the beginner that this work is intended for, you may find that there are parts of this process that come easily and even some that you already know and use, or you might find that all my methods and ideas are new to you. I think of it as sowing a few seeds for you that you can nurture by practising, in order to benefit from more serenity and joy in everyday life, as I seem to be doing at last. At the end of each section are reminders to help you judge your progress, and I recommend that you don't move on until you feel that these points have really been absorbed. In fact, the book is not designed to be rushed through in one go and I urge you to try out the technique in each section, working at it until it becomes a habit. I suggest that you use a new notebook or journal to work through the material and possibly keep a note of any effects you notice.

Because the idea to produce this handbook stemmed from personally offering the material to various groups through presentation, discussion, and exercises, I have tried to maintain the impression of this being a personal one-to-one passing on of ideas, with references to my own experiences, where appropriate. I hope this is helpful. The exercises, which are a vital part of the presentation, are devised from those I have carried out myself during my learning and growth and offered in the classes to others. These classes also involved discussions about our varying experiences and lessons, as well as the beliefs we had developed through these, so I have included some sections on the topics that arose, and other topics that I have contemplated myself. These sometimes include background information that I have learnt, and at other times are simply beliefs I have developed through my inner searches. I offer them here for your consideration or contemplation as occasional intervals while you process the active sections. and to help reinforce your learning.

I wish with all my heart that the opening of this book proves to be the first step in your journey to discovering a more peaceful and happier self within.

# DOES INNER PEACE BRING HAPPINESS?

The quality of the feeling we call happiness may be described by other names. Some that come to mind are contentment, joy, bliss, ecstasy, peacefulness, serenity, relaxation, fun, but, if we look really carefully at these, they all have subtle differences. I have used the word happiness in the sub-title of the book because it seems to be the one most used by those seeking to bring more lightness and positive feeling into their lives. People can be temporarily happy pursuing all manner of activities (or inactivity!) and these invariably depend on external factors being a certain way. We are going to start our quest with this kind of happiness but will be working our way towards finding the kind of happiness that is independent of outside influences and becomes an integral part of who we are, and stays with us whatever the circumstances : i.e. inner peace.

If I were to list for you some of my ideas of what this temporary happiness is, the chances are that you would heartily agree with some and turn up your nose up at others—and maybe even consider me extremely odd. However, I will take that chance and give a few examples in order to get you thinking about a list of your own.

I feel happy when:

- I feel the warm sun on my skin
- I'm enjoying the company of someone I love
- I see beautiful scenery
- I'm paddling in the edge of the surf on a beautiful beach
- I have time to relax at the end of a productive day
- I make someone laugh
- I can help someone physically or emotionally
- I'm learning something interesting
- I'm surrounded by bluebells and trees bursting into leaf
- I hear a blackbird, robin or wren singing...

I could continue at length with topics that help me to feel happy (and what a good exercise that would be for me, as we'll see later) but now I'd like you to start your own list.

* * *

**Exercise 1: Thinking about happiness**

**At this stage, you might not bring very many things to mind. It depends on your state of mind at present and also on how used you are to looking on the brighter side of life. If you have a lot of drama and negativity going on at the moment, it could be very hard for you to summon up the enthusiasm for the exercise. If that is the case, then ask yourself what *used* to make you happy or what *might***

**make you happy in different circumstances. I'd like you to start your list at the top of a blank page so that you have plenty of room to add to the list as items come to mind, which I hope they will do at odd moments throughout your reading. It's also important that you keep this list as we'll be coming back to it when considering other factors in this happiness quest.**

* * *

From this exercise you may notice that the items you and I have listed require certain conditions in the world around us, such as the behaviours of others; having something meaningful to do; our ideal climate; a special place to be, etc. What we are working towards is an ability to feel as we do in these special situations in *any* situation, which may seem like a very big thing to ask but we can get there step by step, by practising some simple techniques every day until we actually rewire our brains to a new attitude and way of being in the world. (I'll explain the biology of it later!) This will enable us to feel such an underlying contentment and sense of security that we no longer look for outside influences to provide these moments of happiness. In fact, we all have access to this within us and we can learn how to reach it at any time, with some pointers and some practice. That's the project we're embarking on here—how to develop a sense of inner peace for any circumstances.

* * *

**Exercise 2: Recognising the feeling of happiness**

**Now I'd like you to take one of the items on your list that you think you can best remember or visualise/imagine. Sit somewhere comfortable and relax your body as well as you can. You'll probably need to close your eyes to bring the situation more vividly to mind and the exercise will work better the more senses you can use by noticing as many as possible of what you see, smell, taste, feel and hear. Imagine yourself there, in the happy situation or with the happy feeling, and notice how your body and mind feel. Try to notice how you feel different from before you were doing the exercise. Please do this exercise before reading on and then see if you agree with the following list.**

* * *

Some of the ways that people describe their feeling of happiness are:

- my body feels relaxed
- my mind is quiet and free of chatter
- I have no negative or disturbing emotions
- I feel contented
- I feel an inner joy

- I feel lighter
- It makes me smile
- I feel kinder towards others.

These all indicate an inner peace.

**NB about the exercises:** Please remember that this book is designed for you to try what has worked for me and the only way to benefit from the reading of it is to carry out the exercises yourself. If you really can't face doing one of them at the time of reading, I recommend that you make a note to come back to it before moving on to the next topic. I have tried to arrange the techniques in the order in which I believe I started to use them.

# RELAXATION FIRST

As human beings we have a large area of our brains (the neo-cortex) devoted to rational thought (and irrational, it must be said!). And don't we know it? During each working day, we think thousands of thoughts, many of them several times over. Of course, we have to give thought to a lot of our activities, and we sometimes have to make plans, but, if we're really honest with ourselves, we know that a huge percentage of our thoughts are just like so many flies buzzing in, out and around our consciousness and over which we apparently have no control. Some random thoughts can bring a smile or happy feeling; others may be worrying, niggling, and causing us that dreaded state—stress.

It is a sad fact that many of the world's current population consider stress as just an occupational hazard of being alive in the 21st century. However, even if there are apparently stressful events taking place around us (and there always are, somewhere), we can still choose to remain calm and peaceful inside—with practice. Not only is this of huge benefit to our own health and welfare, but it can actually help those around us, the situation we are in and, believe it or not, the human race. Yes, if I want more peace in the world, the best place to start creating it is inside myself!

There are various words used as the opposite of stress, such as peace, calm, serenity, but I feel that the real opposite must be relaxation, so we will start with the simple act of relaxing, both physically and mentally.

## LOOSENING EXERCISE

You may well have your own favourite or regular forms of exercise and have discovered the relaxation that follows a good session of that. For our purposes here—and especially if you don't usually exercise—I want you to commit to a small routine as part of this relaxation chapter. I am hoping that you will be able to manage to do your own routine or at least some of the following every day. A relaxed body helps the mind to relax too and can even help to release emotions stored in the body.

Please don't attempt any of these that might cause too much discomfort or adversely affect any existing ailments. If you are not physically able to do any of them, please devise some of your own that enable the loosening of joints and muscles. It is also a fact that even just visualising doing the exercises can be of similar benefit, incredible as that may seem.

* * *

**Exercise 1:**

**Stand up with your feet shoulder-width apart and let both your arms hang loosely by your sides. Now swing both arms from the shoulders around your body to the left and then to the right, keeping them very loose. This will result in the leading arm lightly knocking your back or buttocks and the front arm knocking your abdomen. Do this for at least one minute.**

* * *

**Exercise 2:**

**Still standing, and with your feet shoulder-width apart, joggle your whole body for about a minute. This involves a quick bouncing movement of the legs and torso, with the arms shaking loosely at your sides and your shoulders rising and falling quickly. Consciously loosen your neck and let your head joggle a little, but not so much as to make you dizzy. After the minute, stand still and notice how your body feels.**

* * *

**Exercise 3:**

**Still standing, swing your arms from front to back as when walking but keeping them very loose. Once this motion is established, raise your right arm above your head and let it drop down quickly with a sharp burst of out-breath. Repeat with the left arm. After three on each side, stay still to notice the sensations in your arms.**

* * *

**Exercise 4:**

**In a sitting or lying position, let your attention travel to each part of your body; hold the muscles tense in that area for the count of five and then let them go. Keep your attention on that part of your body for a short while after relaxing it to notice the sensations in it. Right hand; left hand; right shoulder (lift) ; left shoulder (lift) ; face; abdomen; buttocks; right thigh; left thigh; right foot; left foot.**

* * *

These are just a few simple body-loosening exercises to release tension. It's not only physical activities and ailments that cause our bodies to hold tension and become stiff. Very often the stiffness is generated by some of those thousands of thoughts that are assailing us each day, and it can be very surprising and revealing to notice how tightly we are holding some muscles for no apparent reason. One of the habits I would like you to cultivate for this section is to notice from time to time where you hold tension in your body and there follows a very simple practice in exercise 5 to help achieve this.

## STOP AND BREATHE

Aren't we lucky that we've been designed in such a way that most of us don't usually have to think about breathing? Our amazing bodies just get on with the process of taking in air, extracting the oxygen that we need and breathing out the carbon dioxide bi-product that is no use to us. I can't help thinking that, if it were left to me to remember to breathe constantly, the result could vary from very distracting to totally disastrous!

Right now, just stop reading and become aware of your breathing for a minute. Now work your way, sentence by sentence, through the following paragraph, becoming more aware of your breath as you do so.

Let your attention go to the point of entry of that breath—the nostrils or the mouth—and feel the air entering your body on the in-breath. See if you can imagine it making its way down your neck via the windpipe and then branching off into the lungs on both sides of your body, within your ribcage. You might notice that your chest expands and rises as you do this, or you might feel your abdomen expanding, if you're used to belly-breathing. In fact, if you don't already belly-breathe, you could try a few breaths of that now, as it gives your lungs more expansion room in order to take in a bigger ration of fresh air. It simply means letting your abdomen expand as you breathe in, and collapse as you exhale instead of all the action being only in the chest. Watch the out-breath too, noticing how all the areas of the body deflate as the air leaves again through the mouth or nose. You could experiment for a breath or two with breathing just a little more slowly which will almost certainly lead to you taking deeper breaths.

Have you noticed anything else at the end of this experiment? Do you feel any different from before you focused on your breath? Do you remember what you were just reading or thinking about before you started the exercise? The chances are that you are feeling a little calmer than you were before and your head may be clearer.

So, you have just become aware of and followed your breath. Almost all meditation practices use the breath to some extent, some meditators using only a following of the breath in and out of the body to take them to a calm and peaceful state away from thoughts or to what they call an altered state of consciousness. But we are not aiming to go into a deep state of meditation, and this programme is not just another book about how to meditate. We are simply using the breath as a point of focus to bring us from the business of the mind down into the body. The following exercise is a very important first step on the road to *awareness*, which, as I shall explain in the next chapter, is the cornerstone to creating the life of calm we want to achieve.

**Exercise 5: The body scan**

**Using the technique described above, concentrate for a few breaths, watching them going into and out of the body, and noticing how your body does this. After about three breaths, notice other parts of your body, assessing whether they are relaxed or tense. (I often find that I'm holding tension in my shoulders or face.) Try to consciously relax any areas that feel tight by visualising the tension leaving with the out-breath. How long this takes will depend on how stressed you were feeling but, hopefully, it should only be a few minutes.**

So, having done this exercise once to become familiar with the practice, I am now suggesting that you make this part of your everyday life by practising it as often as is possible and practical. In time, you should find that it can often be enough to just stop what you're doing and take one deep breath in and out. A further step in relaxing body and mind when you have been static for a while, if practical, is simply to stand up, walk about a little, noticing your surroundings. This will bring you back to an awareness of your body and any tensions that are there to be released. It need only take a few moments and then you simply carry on with what you were doing. At first you may well need reminders to stop now and then, as we get very caught up in our activities and with other people and—more than anything—in all the myriad thoughts charging through our brains.

I have used various reminders such as:

- stopping on the hour or at a fixed time past the hour
- sticking little notes around the house for me to see
- setting reminders on the mobile phone
- noticing when I'm changing from one activity to another
- when I sit down in the car before I set off
- during the ads on television
- at red lights when driving
- before starting to eat
- visiting the bathroom!

I suggest you spend a few minutes to think up some good memory-joggers for yourself if none of mine suit you and, by the way, unless you are a super top student, I don't advise trying to use all of these. Pick a few to start with. You might be surprised how quickly you get into the habit, and that's the aim.

## REMINDER

**Before you move on to the next chapter, you need to create some habits based on this one:**

1. Do some physical loosening exercise every day, even if for only five minutes, but more if you can manage it.

2. Before you get up each morning, connect with the breath, watching it come and go for at least three breaths.
3. Decide on how you will remind yourself to come back to watching your breath several times a day.
4. Get into the habit of scanning through your body and releasing tension whenever you remember to focus on your breath.

# AWARENESS

Although we're only very early on in this project, we come now to what I believe to be possibly the most important lesson. Once I felt I had fully understood the significance of being truly aware, I felt that anything else was possible because it gave me so much control over my experience of life and all that life could throw at me. You notice that I say 'my experience of life' and not just 'my life'. I know I can't control my life because the unexpected happens so often, but I am at least in charge of how I **perceive** what happens, and I always have a choice about how I **respond** Please notice too that I don't say 'react' but 'respond'. As I'll explain later, we don't have much control over our reactions (which trigger emotions in us) ) because they are often so hard-wired into our brains by our experiences in life, but, if we become consciously aware, it helps us to notice these and, when possible, to respond in a chosen way instead.

What do I mean by being **consciously aware**?

> **A state of being when I am intentionally registering what's going on in my life in this moment within and without. It's a state that enables me to notice what I'm seeing, hearing, feeling, thinking and how I am reacting to it all.**

Of course, we are all aware to a certain degree. At a basic level it equates to noticing things such as the weather; who we're with; where we are and some of what is going on around us. We might be aware of pain in our body or of a worry about something that keeps coming to mind. The degree of awareness that I have found so life-altering and enhancing takes us a bit deeper than this and takes some practice to achieve as a natural way of being. Believe me, it is very worth the effort.

Conscious awareness enables us to notice:

- how our body is feeling—where we're holding tension and blocking energy
- our reactions, neuroses and repeating patterns that cause us to behave in certain ways
- these same things in others
- the effect we're having on others
- emotions that are arising, preferably before they go out of control and take us over

We can be consciously going about our everyday life without being aware. Our body functions with all its systems up and running. We move about and do things, some requiring attention and thought, but a lot happening automatically while our thoughts are elsewhere. You might like to imagine the following scenarios that, I hope, will illustrate the state of awareness that I want us to aim for.

- **Walking:** I go for a walk on the coast in the sunshine and let my mind wander where it will, possibly worrying, fretting, reliving stressful events and conversations.

OR

I walk the coast enjoying the feel of the sun on my skin and noticing how it glints on the water, creates interesting shadows, and lights up the corn fields I pass. I feel the touch of my clothes as I walk. I notice how my body feels, and relax any tensions that I find. I see and appreciate the myriad wild flowers and hear the various birds singing and calling. I notice white puffy clouds against the blue sky and feel the hint of a breeze on my face. I smell the freshness of the air. I feel my feet connecting to the path I'm walking and am aware of gravity keeping me anchored as well as the way my body balances as I go. I am also aware of my emotions as I walk.

- **Eating:** I sit down to eat my meal with something to read or the television on and before long I notice that I've finished it.

OR

I sit down with my meal, noticing how hungry I am, and take a few breaths while appreciating its appearance on the plate—the colours, textures and variety of it. I notice the smell of it. If I feel inclined, I can be aware of the journey the food has made from plant to plate, and the people involved in bringing it to me. Then, as I take each mouthful, I really notice its smell, taste, and texture in my mouth as I chew. I swallow each mouthful before preparing the next, giving each the same attention. I notice any emotions that arise while I'm eating.

These examples are probably far more detailed than most of us can (or even want to) achieve, but hopefully give you some idea of what full awareness would feel like. It's interesting to consider how far from this extreme we usually are when carrying out these everyday activities. This type of practice is sometimes called 'mindfulness','being present' or 'in the present moment' and there is a lot of literature and various courses devoted to cultivating this way of being. The idea is that being this way brings us away from the incessant babble of thoughts occupying our brains every second of the day, often causing us stress. I can vouch for the fact that this does really work but we have to make gradual progress. So, here's my next little practice for you to try.

## HERE I AM (CHECKING-IN)

First of all, we need to establish who I mean by 'I' in this case and this will be easier for some than others, possibly depending on your beliefs. Have you ever noticed, as I have, that it feels as if you're having a conversation or argument in your head between two parts of yourself? I've come to think of them as my ego and my **real self**. My ego is the personality self who gets on with everyday life according to what living on Earth requires, whereas the **real me** is the part that only I really know. It's the part of me who watches everything that happens around me and within me. Some call it my soul, higher self, spirit, consciousness, the observer, etc. I've found that the **real me** is always calm and peaceful while the ego/personality goes up and down, round and round, constantly reacting with the events in life. Rather like the water of a lake—the water on the surface gets blown and tossed into waves while, underneath, all is calm and peaceful. So, in the following exercises, try to get in touch with that **real** part of yourself.

**Exercise 1:**

**First of all, just sit quietly and connect with your body, as you've been practising. Consider how there's a part of you deep inside that other people never see, that no-one can possibly really know how you feel inside. This part of you has a huge store of memories that only you can access, with all the feelings they evoke. Notice how you cannot escape being the *real you* until the day you die. You can take lots of different roles; put on faces and acts; behave according to the circumstances, but it's still you in there experiencing everything in your own unique way.**

**Now, as you sit there, think of your *real self* as you say to yourself: "*Here I am*, sitting in this chair, getting in touch with the *real me*." Notice how you are sitting, what you're wearing and things around you, really concentrating on being the *real you*. Then get up and walk slowly about the room. Think or say to yourself things like:"*Here I am* walking around the room. I'm looking at this picture. I'm picking up this book. I'm sitting back on the chair."**

Don't worry if you don't feel that you're getting this yet. It might take a while. If you can, just trust that there is a calm and peaceful self within you who doesn't get caught up in the turmoil of life and that you can sink down into this self when you need to. We are aiming to bring our attention back to our body and the present moment, away from any thoughts and activities that may be causing us agitation. Saying to yourself "Here I am", together with focusing on a couple of breaths and the body, is quick, simple and can be done anywhere at any time. It's relaxing and releasing, and the beginning of **awareness**.

The idea now is to combine your breathing breaks with saying to yourself "Here I am" and making that connection with the inner you - the **real you**.

Here's an example of how I started with this process:**Chopping veg**:I used to often find, when chopping vegetables for dinner, that my mind was usually busy anywhere but in the kitchen with me. (We'll look very shortly at some of the places our minds go off to, because they are the biggest obstacle to having a calm, peaceful and happy life.) Having decided that awareness and mindfulness were skills I wanted to acquire, I found this a great opportunity to come back to the present moment. I'd just stop for a few seconds and invariably discovered that my shoulders were lifted and tense and that I was breathing shallowly and only into my chest rather than my belly. I still do the exercise now by stopping, taking a couple of breaths, and saying to myself "Here I am, chopping veg". First, I check through my body and release any tension I find and then I think about the vegetables I'm chopping and the meal I'm making. Sometimes I find it helpful to expand this into stopping for a bit longer and looking around at my kitchen and out of the window, taking in everything around me. This really brings me back to the real me and the present moment. I become aware of everything in that moment that is happening inside me and in my environment. You might like to try this or a variation of it for any other activity and there are other little additions that you can add that increase the feeling of presence and well-being.

**Exercise 2: The 'here I am' exercise**

1. **Stop the activity you are currently doing.**
2. **Take two deep breaths and notice where your mind is.**
3. **Now take your attention to your body and release any tension you find.**
4. **Say to yourself "Here I am doing... (whatever the activity is) " and get in touch with the real you.**
5. **Bring your mind back to focus on the activity (even if it's the inactivity of listening to someone or something).**
6. **Look around at your surroundings.**
7. **Keep breathing deeply and smile.**
8. **Feel grateful for something in your life that comes to mind.**
9. **Tell yourself that you are feeling calm and peaceful.**

Choose little activities at first and use your breathing reminders until you get into the habit and can extend the awareness to longer periods.

Here are a few more occasions that can be used for this practice:

- waiting in a queue
- waiting for your computer to boot
- watching television
- having a cup of tea or coffee
- sitting on the toilet
- washing up
- filling the car with fuel
- any gardening or housework activity.

It might be that you don't like the actual words 'here I am' and you prefer to find your own phrase. I have friends who say things such as 'checking in', 'be still', 'be still and know that I am' or 'stop and breathe'. Whatever you decide on, make sure that it connects you with your breath, your body and your real self by completing the exercise as above. This ensures that you get into the calm and peaceful part of you who is totally present in the moment. It's the first step towards cultivating conscious awareness.

## REMINDERS

**By now I hope you are remembering the following practices at least a few times each day:**

1. loosening exercises
2. stopping to take a few deep breaths
3. scanning your body and releasing any tension you find.

**I would now like you to add the following, and get into the habit of doing all of these before you move on to the next section. Please remember that the secret to succeeding with this programme is to make these practices into habits *gradually* so that they become a natural part of how you live your life, so please don't move on until you feel these habits forming:**

4. the 'here I am' exercise as often as you can
5. carrying out at least one activity each day with as much awareness as possible.

# PREVENTION AND CURE

I hope you've had some success by now with the 'here I am' exercise so that it's becoming a regular habit throughout the day. You should also now be more in touch with your body and able to find and release any tensions that you hold in it. Hopefully your shoulders stay relaxed, you breathe more deeply and slowly, and your face stays softer, frequently offering a smile to yourself and the world. If this last sentence is a bit too optimistic, then at least I hope you are noticing when these things are not happening. That's half the battle and you can congratulate yourself that you are becoming more **aware**!

I know only too well that, at this stage, it can be a real struggle to stay aware and that, when we do remember to come back to our real selves, our breathing, and our bodies, we find all sorts of distractions, tensions, worries have been occupying us. The two temptations then are to scold ourselves for failing in our practice, or to blame others or our circumstances and fear that, because of the latter, this scheme isn't going to work for us.

Please don't be disheartened. I'm not saying that you should be able to stay constantly aware, calm and peaceful by now. It is still very early days, and we have the habits of years to overcome. We have been a lifetime so far laying down the neural pathways in our brains that make us who we are today and this is not going to change overnight. It's important to be patient and kind to yourself while continuing to practise as often as possible and also to believe firmly that you are fully capable of achieving success.

Now we must take a close look at where we find our mind has wandered to instead of it staying aware of the present moment and current activity. A lot of the time in our daily lives we are operating on 'automatic pilot' while our mind is off in a world of its own, possibly down memory lane or in a fantasy land of its own making. Whatever the emotions may be within this fantasy land of the mind, they are having an effect on our bodies over which we are taking no conscious control, and this is not a helpful state of affairs. Remember that it is a scientific fact that emotions are felt by every cell in the body, and electrical, chemical, and hormonal changes take place accordingly. Amazingly, this applies whether the scenario is real or imagined! Therefore, what we think, and feel is bound to have a physical effect on us, making it even more important that we personally have control over this.

## THE PREVENTERS

So, let's look at what prevents us from staying calm, peaceful and present all the time. We will see them as outside influences of course—people and circumstances—but it's really our *relationship* to what happens in our life that causes how we feel. We always have *choice* about this but, unless we are aware of our thoughts and the emotions that these are generating, and have strategies to deal with them, we can feel pretty helpless and end up suffering.

I am aware here that the above paragraph will represent a very big step in understanding for some readers, such as believing that we each have a real self within, who is always calm and peaceful and that we can contact at will, we must believe that we can *choose* how to respond to outside influences. I think it's fair to say that the most commonly held belief is that other people and our circumstances are what cause us to feel a certain way and to have certain reactions. Well, if we are not fully aware of what is going on within us, these factors will govern how we react and behave, but with the knowledge that we can change the habits, beliefs and perceptions that no longer serve us, we can become the masters of our own lives.

If you are finding yourself resistant to this idea, please don't worry. Almost everyone does at first, but once grasped, I believe it to be one of the most crucial turning points in this process. When I began to get the hang of noticing my reactions—always after the event in the early days—and thinking about how I could have responded differently, it was such an awakening, and I could see the potential for far greater serenity in my life. With practice, of course, it becomes easier to see what's going on earlier in a situation and to behave thoughtfully at the time.

Here are some of **my preventers** as examples—things that used to or still do threaten to make me lose my calm:

- worrying about an event I'm not looking forward to (future)

- being with people I find difficult, or thinking about others' lives (others)
- wishing I had said or done something differently (past)
- wondering whether I'm being good enough, or wanting to be right (me/ego)
- wishing I weren't cold (fighting reality)
- running over 'to do' lists in my head (busyness).

**Exercise 1:**

1. **Just stop reading for a moment and sit, letting your mind wander.**
2. **After a few minutes, notice where it's gone and make a note.**
3. **Now reflect for a while on what other things often fill your mind or upset you, and list a few of them.**
4. **Notice whether any of yours are similar to my examples.**

## CATEGORIES

As you can see, I've put each of my examples into a category, which we'll now go on to explore in more detail.

a) **Past**:
   - regretting something you've said or done
   - reliving an unpleasant experience

- o wondering about how things could have been different
- o reliving a happy experience in a regretful way.

Obviously, there isn't always a problem with happy thoughts about the past and they can be useful for helping us to feel calm, as long as we're not letting ourselves be sad that they are past and not present.

**b) Future:**

- o planning ahead in a vague way
- o dreaming/fantasizing
- o worrying about a future event or outcome.

**c) You/others:**

- o caught up in the activities of the outside world
- o judging others' behaviour
- o too interested in others' affairs
- o trying to change others
- o worrying about other people (most likely those closest to us)
- o blaming others for how you feel.

**d) Me/ego:**

- o too conscious of what others think of me
- o over-striving to be better, get well, achieve some goal
- o wanting to be liked/loved
- o feeling that I don't matter or am unappreciated.

**e) Fighting reality:**

- o our emotional reactions to circumstances, people, events, either current or permanent, and wanting them to be different.

f) **Busyness**
  - o believing that we have to be actively doing something all the time
  - o racing against time
  - o forgetting that we are human beings
  - o going over mental 'to do' lists.

**Exercise 2:**

1. **Look again at my list of preventers and see how I've categorised them.**
2. **See if you can categorise your own list.**
3. **Write out the headings big and bold in your journal to help you learn them.**
4. **Each time you do 'here I am', notice where your mind was previously and work out which 'preventer' was keeping it busy and away from the present moment.**

When we go on to the next section, you can extend the exercise to see which of the 'cures' will work for you to bring you back to calm and peacefulness, but you need to create the habit of noticing the 'preventers' first, before thinking about curing them. You will find that just stopping to notice where your thoughts have gone, and working out the category, combined with a few deep breaths, is often enough to bring some peace and calm.

## LOOKING DEEPER AT SOME PREVENTERS AND THE OBJECTIONS TO THEM

I can understand—and almost hear!—some readers' objections to some of these preventers being curable, or even needing to be. Don't forget I've been through all this learning too (and am still learning, of course!). At this stage, you may well find resistance to stopping some chains of thoughts and might want to remain wherever your thoughts have taken you. Just don't forget that we are tip-toeing our way to staying calm and peaceful, no matter what, and to achieve this we have to discover what helps and what hinders us. Don't be surprised if your reaction at this point is not to want to prevent your thoughts going off in these various directions. You are not alone, and it's not surprising with such a radical idea as this is—that we take control of our thoughts rather than letting them control us.

It helps to remember that we are not our thoughts. They come into our mind, and our real self can see and categorise them as an observer would. From this position we can see what they do to us via our emotions, and then choose whether to let this continue or to prevent it. I liken it to eating or drinking something that makes us feel sick. In our conscious, reasoning state we can choose what we eat and drink, and I think it safe to say that most of us would not choose to make ourselves ill or taste something horrible. So why let these intruding thoughts disturb our serenity and prevent us enjoying all that's good in our lives? I'll offer a few words now about some of the stumbling blocks that I've come across, and others will be covered as we progress.

## PAST

**If we've had happy times, why not relive them?**

No reason at all, and it can do us a lot of good both emotionally and physically. My only warning is not to let this distract from what's good in the present. There is always a danger, too, of comparison creeping in and causing discontent with present circumstances when we look back at happy times. If you find this happening, it's no longer having a beneficial effect. If possible, feel gratitude for the past and then find things to be grateful for in the present.

## FUTURE

**Why shouldn't I let my thoughts take me ahead to a weekend outing while I'm driving home on a Thursday night? It might help me face another tricky/boring/worrying/hard day at work tomorrow.**

Well, there may be a few dangers here, although they are not always present. It might indeed make you feel good to let your imagination roam and might be worth the 'risk' for a while. However, do watch out for:

a) how the human mind has a way of looking for trouble and you could find yourself focusing on what could go wrong with the future event or what arrangements still need to be made or thought about, all of which could cause tension.

b) building up an image of how a future event will be, i.e. fantasising, can lead to disappointment if it doesn't actually happen or doesn't come up to our expectations. My experience has been that expectations are often a cause of suffering. It's probably best to avoid such practices until you've mastered always accepting how things turn out.

Don't forget that, while you're away in the future, you are not really living the present moment and appreciating all that it has to offer. You are living in an imaginary world while the real one passes you by.

Of course, we often do have to think ahead in order to function in our busy world, and we do have to make some short- and long-term plans. I deal with the planning in the 'Cures' section. As for just thinking ahead, my experience is that we can get carried away too far, either into scenarios that might never happen or into strings of jobs and 'to do' lists, and find ourselves overwhelmed and stressed. Just watch out for such happenings. Your body's tensing muscles may warn you when this occurs.

## OTHERS

**Well, of course we want to think about others in positive ways and we have to do so with those in our care.**

Try to keep these thoughts positive and beware of obsessing about anyone or any situation—a recipe for distraction and stress. If you've been asked for advice by someone, it's probably best to set aside time to give this some serious thought rather than letting your thoughts wander around aimlessly.

Additionally, if you are fretting over something that's happened and find you are blaming someone for how you feel, you are slipping into victimhood. This is both stressful and disempowering for you. Because we can't change what's happened, or other people, we can only look, and deal with, our own reactions, and acknowledge how we are feeling. This enables us to learn more about ourselves in order to move on in a better frame of mind.

## EGO (FRIEND OR FOE?)

Looking out for, and working on, these preventers is a very big step for us. It can be a revelation to watch what our mind is up to all day, and the way it affects how we feel. If we feel no peace, joy, or love as a result of our thoughts, it must be our ego/personality that is behind them, as our real self is our peaceful centre. So, ego is another aspect that we need to stay aware of. Of course, we need to operate in the world through our ego/personality most of the time, but this part of us can be responsible for a lot of our negative thoughts and behaviours, such as competition, revenge, righteousness, anger. In relation to others, it might want to be better in some way such as cleverer, wealthier, prettier or right.

I hope this helps with some of the preventers that you feel resistance to. Later topics will deal with some of the others but, for the moment, please try to notice them arising and accept that bringing yourself back to the here and now is a vital step in improving your awareness.

## THE CURES

What a relief to know that there are cures for each of these preventers and all we must do is get into the habit of recognising the preventers and applying the cures. The first step is to become aware of the mind's wanderings through awareness, maybe noticing body tension. Then say mentally to your mind "Come back" and look at where it's been. For the preventers above, these are the cures that I use:

**Past, future, me:** Come into the present–come back from the past and the future and into the current activity and the real me. Be in the present moment. I know that there are things we do have to plan and review but even that can be done in an aware, present, and centred way. When I notice that the past and future creep in to disturb my calm and they are subjects that do have to be thought about, my trick is to say to myself "Not now. I'll think about that later", knowing that I will set aside time to give that matter my full attention.

**You/others:** Go back to my centre: stay centred in my own body and experience. Body awareness helps with this. We must remember that we are not here to change others. This is impossible anyway, as they would change only if and when they wanted to. For this one I say to myself "It's none of my business". Parents obviously cannot ignore what is going on with their children, and we want to have care and compassion for others, but this does not have to be in a worrying way. I've noticed that parents of grown-up offspring can waste a lot of time and energy and get themselves very agitated by not being able to let their children live and grow through their own mistakes and successes.

It could be, of course, that for your own or others' sake or safety, you do have to take some action involving others, in which case you might need to set aside time to research and find out what support there is to help you. The important thing is to take that action rather than letting your thoughts swirl around, causing more stress.

**Fighting reality:** Act, leave or accept. To surrender and **allow** life to unfold is the ideal but this is not always easy. Feeling calm and peaceful and living from the real me allows more wisdom through and we make better decisions. We can either take **action** to correct the situation that we don't want; we may be able to **leave** the situation; or sometimes we have to decide, for the sake of our own serenity, to **accept** things just as they are rather than keep resisting. Remember that nothing stays the same forever. "This too shall pass" can be a helpful thought at difficult times.

**Busy-ness:** Slow down and be. Remember that what matters more than what we do is **how** we are when doing it, and that we want to be peaceful beings. Notice whether your busyness is a way to avoid looking deeply into a feeling, behaviour, or situation that you don't want to face. Dealing with our strong emotions is something we shall move on to later. At this stage, we need to do our best to become as peaceful as we can by coming back into our body and breath ('checking-in') and concentrating on the present moment. Pull back your scattered mind by repeating "Here I am".

**All of them:** Stay aware of thoughts and feelings. Notice your reactions (spot and stop). Become aware of physical and emotional tensions, and more accepting of them. It's very important not to beat ourselves up about any of these but to see each preventer that we notice as an opportunity to learn more about ourselves and to practise responding in more helpful ways.

## LOOKING A BIT DEEPER AGAIN

### WORRYING

Several of the preventers involve worrying about people and events and I'm not sure that many of us realise the futility of worrying. It is a damaging occupation that most of us have done or do a lot of over the course of a lifetime. Now that science has shown what a real effect our thoughts and emotions have on our bodies, and hence our health and fitness, we must see that worrying, as a negative emotion, is physically harming ourselves. For example, imagine that you have a dental appointment coming up that sounds as if it could be quite an ordeal. Option one is to create in your mind all sorts of painful and difficult scenarios about how it will go, such as that you could have terrible pain; there might be a lot of blood that won't stop quickly; it might take a very long time; you might feel awful afterwards and not be able to eat or drink for ages.

Option two is to put it out of your mind each time it creeps in and remind yourself that whatever is going to happen need only happen once, not over and over again in your imagination. Otherwise, with option one, you are putting your body through a trauma each time you imagine it. The thing to do when worrying about the future is to say to yourself "Not now". In this case it's a reminder that this is not happening now. If you are worrying about something you need to plan or organise, then you're telling yourself that you will set aside time later to focus on and deal with the issue.

Many top athletes and their coaches have proven how effective is the process of visualisation (what we are doing in option one). Incredibly it has been found that our subconscious cannot tell the difference between visualising something and actually doing it. Even muscle power can be improved by imagining in detail some action. So, when we imagine something unpleasant happening to us, our subconscious sets in motion all the bodily reactions that it would in the real event, thus unnecessarily distressing the body.

With awareness in the above situation, we would notice the tension building during the imagined scenario, because of the chemicals and hormones that would be running to the rescue, and this would enable us to choose the healthier option two.

## PLANNING

I often find myself distracted by my thoughts about some future event that isn't necessarily a worry but nevertheless takes me away from enjoying the present moment or distracts me into busyness or even making mistakes. This can be something like preparing to go away; or for having visitors, and I start making mental lists of what needs to be done. This can be another case for saying "Not now" and setting the intention to sit down and give the matter all my attention at some future time, with pen and paper at the ready. Or it may be that it suits me to think something through while doing something else, such as going for a walk to think over factors concerning a decision I must make. In the latter case, I have made that decision with awareness and not just let my monkey mind take over the walk.

## REGRETTING

If regrets are the distraction and cause of bad feelings, then we must choose to either take some action or to change how we think about what happened. Either way, there is nothing to be gained by beating ourselves up about our words or actions, nor about stewing on those of someone else, when we could be enjoying some peace in the present moment. There may be some forgiving to be done for self or other (more about forgiveness later), apologies to be made or some frank discussion to be faced, in which case we need to make a commitment to carry out one of these at the appropriate time and for the moment put the matter out of our head. On the other hand, it might be that nothing can be done to remedy the situation and, obviously, the past can't be changed. When the regretful thoughts are out of control and causing stress, I find it's best to deal with the issue in a mindful way which, for me, means setting aside some time to look at what I can learn from the situation.

**The important thing to remember is that we only need to use a cure when our**

**peace of mind has been disrupted or we are feeling emotionally upset or physically affected by a preventer. There are obviously times when we have to plan ahead, and I have found that the best method is to allot time to doing the planning in an organised way and with awareness.**

## RESISTING

Another very common preventer (probably the most common) is 'fighting reality'. I have listed three cures for this—act, leave or accept. Of course, it's best to consider first whether we can change in a harmonious way the situation that's causing us grief. It's important to remember in this case, though, that we can't change anyone else involved in it and we shouldn't try. We are here to live our own life, not someone else's!A lovely wisdom I've learnt from a Susan Jeffers book is not to be concerned with why someone acts the way they do but to look at my reaction to that.

So, if changing the situation is not possible, would leaving it be the wisest move for our own peace of mind (such as if we are finding someone difficult to be with, or we are uncomfortable in a certain place or atmosphere)? I have found this useful when witnessing disagreements among others in my space. It's too easy to get drawn into the argument as a witness or conspirator!It isn't always possible to leave the scene physically, but we can refuse to get emotionally involved, either by stating out loud that we are not taking part or by making a conscious decision to focus on something else and not be drawn in emotionally.

If neither changing nor leaving is possible or desirable, then acceptance is the decision of choice. The actual carrying out of this option may require just a simple decision to get on with the job in hand, or resign oneself to the situation. On the other hand, it might be a real battle with the emotions in order to keep bringing the thoughts back from their place of resistance and creating a fresh feeling of calm that comes from acceptance. Rest assured that we can get better at this with practice.

Again, when we fight reality (put up a resistance to what is) we are creating tension and stiffness in the body somewhere. Think of a puppy or a donkey who refuses to move on when requested—how stiff they make themselves in their stubbornness! There has to be a degree of this taking place inside the human who refuses to accept. Because it is such a common trait to fight reality, I recommend that you notice it and practise the cure to start with on daily resistances such as wishing for different weather; wanting not to be ill; being impatient in queues; wishing Monday morning were Saturday instead; not wanting to have to do a certain necessary chore.

In addition to these cures for resistance, there is usually a need to look at why we are not happy with a situation, and this is another exercise for those who are ready to undertake the work. However, in the moment, and as an initial step, it's worth just developing an awareness of how we are feeling.

**Exercise 3:**

**Read through the following scenario part (a). Then close your eyes and picture yourself in the situation with all the emotion you can muster (this little bit won't do the body any lasting harm!).**

**(a) You're in the car driving to an important appointment and come up to the back of a traffic jam. Your heart sinks, slight panic sets in about being late. You're cross that you didn't choose a different route. Nothing's moving ahead and you feel trapped.**

**Notice how your body has reacted to the emotions you experienced.**

**Now read part (b), visualising yourself behaving in that way and letting its effect work on you as you read it.**

**(b) Now awareness kicks in. You check in by dropping your shoulders, take three deep slow breaths and check your body for other tensions such as a tight tummy or clenched jaw or hands. You realise that you're fighting reality, notice your posture and your contact with the seat and your**

**clothes touching your body. You bring yourself back to the present by looking around at and really noticing the verges, noticing the weather and whatever's around—the different vehicles, scenery, buildings, people, colours. You take some more slow breaths, smile think of something that makes you happy, and appreciate this time to relax and centre yourself. You take the opportunity to reflect on the futility of fighting against something that you can't change and the 'insanity' of causing yourself internal stress and damage.**

## RECAP: HOW I DO IT (USING THE CURES)

When I become aware that I have some tension (when my body tells me usually) or when my thoughts are going wild, I stop what I'm doing, relax my shoulders or whatever parts of me have become tense, take a few breaths, and then take remedial action, starting by asking myself a question:

### Am I in the past or future?

If so, I come back to the present activity. I can't change the past but I can learn from it so I can set an intention to do something differently next time. If worries are stealing my calm, I say to them "Not now", reminding myself that these imagined happenings are not real and may never be. If it's something that I need to give attention to, the 'not now' means that I'll give it attention at a specific time. It can also be something that has come to mind needing my immediate attention, in which case I take action there and then, even if it just involves writing something down so that I don't forget it later.

**Am I judging, worrying about someone else or trying to change them?**

In this case, I'm in the 'you' preventer, which I cure by saying to myself "It's none of my business. I can only live my own life and let them live theirs".

**Am I concerned about what others are thinking of me?**

I need to concentrate on the present activity and just be myself. Again, it's none of my business what others think of me. We can't please or be attractive to everyone as we all have such different tastes and opinions, so why waste time trying? (The 'Self-esteem' section will deal with this in more depth.)

**Am I fighting reality?**

Can I take action, leave the situation or must I accept?

**Am I trying to achieve too much?**

I have to look at why I am pushing myself and remember to breathe and just **be** now and then. I also need to remind myself that moving slowly and with awareness often gets more done in less time and more efficiently. In fact, deliberately doing something slowly and carefully that you would normally rush through can feel very calming, but I appreciate that this might be something that needs to be worked on gradually.

**Staying with it** because our aim at this stage is to notice what is destroying our tranquillity and hence our happiness, this section has been giving you ways of regularly coming back to the real you and your peaceful, calm centre. However, I am aware that there are times when we need to deal with a feeling that has surfaced. Facing and dealing with our emotions are the ways we grow and learn about ourselves. That's why I suggest that you work only on the minor items at this stage. We will look at ways of working with the bigger issues later on. Reading the 'Thoughts on Thoughts' section that follows may increase your determination to stay aware of what your mind is up to.

## REMINDERS

1. I hope that 'here I am'/'checking in' is now a habit. If not, please don't move on yet.
2. You now need to add the process of checking what prevents you from being calm and peaceful and learn and practise the appropriate cures. See how you fare over the next week or so before going on to the next practical section. Don't expect wonders with the big issues. Aim to notice and deal with some of the everyday small irritations that nevertheless take away your calm.

**By all means read the 'Thoughts on thoughts' that follow, or some positive reading matter from the appendix.**

# THOUGHTS ON THOUGHTS—ARE THEY YOUR FRIENDS OR ENEMIES?

Let's take a close look at why we need to be constantly aware of our thoughts. After all, we are not our thoughts and emotions. They happen to us, and we can be the observer of them, through awareness, rather than letting them control or disturb us.

As you look around you now, notice how so much of what you see started as a single thought. Every manufactured object was thought into existence by someone who had to have the idea to put into practice. Even our use of invisible things such as electricity was made possible by someone thinking about how to harness it, use it and then how to make it available to us. This is the power of creative thought.

Now reflect briefly on your current position—where you live, your family, your work, your friends, your interests. How did you arrive where you are in life now? Most likely by making hundreds of decisions along your way, all fuelled by millions of thoughts, a lot of which will have been about whether something was/is good or bad, better or worse, wise or foolish. Some thoughts we listen to and act upon while others we let go as unhelpful. We are constantly making choices in our material and practical lives, using the power of thought.

But what about our inner, emotional lives? Here too almost everything starts with a thought. Emotions rarely just happen without a thought. Sometimes it's obvious, such as a thought about a planned event bringing excitement and joy, or bad news causing sadness or fear. At other times we might not be so aware of why we are feeling a particular emotion. When the result of this is that we feel stressed, unhappy, anxious, angry, fearful or in any way uncomfortable, we need to find the thought or thoughts that triggered it, because we need to master what goes on in our mind rather than letting it control us. We need to take back our power because it's what we need to use to overcome obstacles to our serenity.

Let's look at what I mean by this personal power. We use it to make our wishes and choices a reality and to live by what we believe. We all have it, and it enables us to create the lives we want. At the time of the 'big bang', when the universe began, power started expanding outwards, and, according to the scientists, it is still doing so. Everything that exists has its origins in that explosion, so we must have some of that power/energy within us. If your belief is rather that an almighty being created the universe and humanity, it still makes sense that we have been endowed with the same creative ability ('in His image') i.e. power. The evidence all around us proves that it is a creative power so we must have it too.

How do we use this power? (I don't mean physical energy or strength, by the way, but an inner ability to make things happen.) Our thoughts will be our friends or enemies in the use of this creative ability depending on whether we keep them positive or allow negative thoughts to assail us. Our subconscious will believe whatever we tell it, so we have to beware (be aware!).

When a thought occurs in the brain, an electrical connection is made between synapses. This may be a single thought or go on to become a whole chain of new or revisited old thoughts. However long the electrical event is, it never happens alone. There is always a consequence because the body responds to every thought in some way by releasing hormones and/or other chemicals into our bodies. All the time we are awake, thoughts are triggering happenings in our bloodstream that affect every cell in our body. I find it a rather alarming fact, but it does encourage me to be as aware as possible of what is going on in this busy mind of mine.

Let's take as an example the thought that it's time to get up in the morning. The brain reacts to the thought by sending messages, via the nervous system, to the muscles that will be involved in getting us out of bed. Apart from the obvious arm, leg, back and neck muscle messages, there will be instructions to heart and lungs to prepare for action, and all of this mostly happens without our conscious awareness. An able-bodied person doesn't usually need to think it through in detail. It's a habit and a reflex reaction to the thought.

Now imagine it's a Monday morning and you are getting out of bed to face the week at a job you hate or dread. The thought about getting your body up and moving will probably be accompanied by others such as wishing you could stay in bed; regrets that the weekend is over; longing to change your job or retire; worries about the duties or relationships you'll be facing during the day. These thoughts as well are having just as much effect on your body. Stress chemicals are being released, muscles tensed, nerves getting into action and other reactions being set up, all of which are not helpful to creating a feeling of well-being. In fact, too much stress chemical being released can have detrimental long-term results and this is what we want to prevent.

This is where our power comes in. It's the power within the real self. This real self knows deep down who I really am and is able to make the wisest choices for my life; choices that protect me from harm and ensure my well-being. This part of me wants to prevent me engaging in activities—and thoughts—that are not in my best interest.

It might be easier to think about how we can lose this power to other people if we let them dominate us directly or if we react to their behaviours in a negative way by letting ourselves be upset by them. We lose our power to them, too, if we act in ways that are not true to our integrity in order to please them. We might abandon our own truth or standards in an effort to keep their approval or love. I'm sure that most of us can think of occasions when we've allowed such things to happen and can remember the uncomfortable, low, deflated feelings this produced in us.

Another way we can lose our power is to give into unhelpful thoughts that lead us to experience negative emotions.

Thoughts flood into the mind in accordance with old habits, beliefs and conditioning that might no longer serve us. These thoughts and the feelings they invoke in us bubble up from the subconscious, unbidden and uncensored. We need to use the power of our conscious, objective self (the real me) to assess the accuracy of these thoughts and, if they are causing us unnecessary stress, to remove or change them.

It is through our thoughts that we create both our present and future life, so it is vitally important that we take control of them. As we become more aware of what our mind is up to and watch where our thoughts have wandered off to, we will see that so much of what we are thinking is purely hypothetical. We make up worrying scenarios about what is happening or is going to happen to ourselves or our loved ones. We create stories about outcomes. We waste valuable time and energy on regrets and wishing we could rewrite past events. A lot of nervous energy can be wasted, and unhappiness caused when we wish that things, circumstances, people could be different because we've deemed our current reality to be bad or wrong. If these can't be changed, we are just causing ourselves more suffering. And we don't just go to these places once but circle round and around in them.

The longer we've been letting our minds get away with this unhelpful behaviour, the more vigilant and determined we have to become in order to take back control. What we have to remember is that we do have the means to achieve this. What we physically have to do is create new pathways in the brain along which the more helpful, positive thoughts will flow. It can be done, and is a method used by many successful people already in fields of sport, business, the arts and other activities where improved performance is required. Our aim is to improve our performance in dealing with the stresses of everyday life and to create ourselves islands of tranquillity in this busy world. What could be more important and beneficial than learning how to remain calm and peaceful within, whatever happens to us in life?

I find that understanding the science helps, combined with visualising it in simple terms, so I think of my thoughts travelling down routes in my brain and finding connections and links to old pre-trodden pathways. This enables them to run wild and to keep making me feel and/or behave in the same old ways that are not always helpful to me. To remedy this, I have to create roadblocks and build new routes or put in diversions. Ideally, I simply block any thoughts I notice that are causing me to feel bad, but it's not that easy—well, not for me!

I do have one friend who says that, if something makes him feel bad, he just doesn't think about it, but I do wonder.

I say it's not easy but, very importantly, it is certainly possible. This is what all those high performers do and it's just down to practice. Some of the old neural pathways will be strong and well formed, like big main roads that will take a while to block off and demolish, and our new routes may be comparatively weak to start with, like narrow country lanes, but we can widen and strengthen these by working on them and travelling along them as often as possible. If you find this image helpful, then make up your mind now to give up the big unattractive highways that you are in the habit of using (thought pathways that cause stress or unhappiness) and start widening and reinforcing the pretty country lanes of positive thoughts that lead to desirable emotions.

Once we learn to watch our thoughts from our real selves, we will also notice the emotions they produce and will realise the benefits of switching from the stress-creating ones to the life-enhancing thoughts. In fact, we can get so good at controlling what we think that we can be constantly creating peaceful, happy feelings throughout our being, which is not only delightful for us to experience but enhances the lives of those around us and, ultimately, the human race as a whole.

Of course, this does only relate to unhelpful thoughts and not to the deeper, subconscious emotions that can surface from past experiences, often even from childhood. These need to be dealt with too, once we feel strong enough, and maybe with the support of a trusted friend or therapist.

# A BIT MORE BREATHING (OR LET'S TAKE A BREATHER)

I'm hoping that by now you will agree that, in order to achieve the peace we seek, we have to learn to avoid or relieve stress as it arises. In other words, we have to be able to stay calm and peaceful as much as possible. This doesn't mean that we won't feel emotions but that we will, through awareness, notice how they are affecting us and respond accordingly. At this stage, we need to aim at returning to calm and peacefulness as often as possible, and we can use breathing techniques a lot to help us with this. I find it very comforting that something as available and as simple as the breath can be such an excellent tool in this endeavour. I hope that by now you are in the habit of taking little breathers frequently throughout your day and using the breath to connect you to your body. Here are some more exercises that I find useful at various times. See which ones suit you best and try to remember to use them whenever you can.

**Exercise 1: belly-breathing—the healthier way to breathe**

1. Take a breath in, directing the air to the area below your navel, and notice your abdomen expand (thus making maximum use of your lungs).
2. Then pull in the abdomen to expel the stale air.
3. Practise this often until it becomes the natural way to breathe.

* * *

**Exercise 2: conscious breathing**

1. Sitting in a relaxed position, send your attention to where the air enters your body.
2. Notice the coolness of it as it passes through your nostrils or mouth.
3. Visualise the breath travelling from the back of your throat, down the windpipe.
4. Notice your lungs expanding, from the belly upwards if possible, and how they change from expanding to relaxing.
5. Feel the slightly warmer air leaving through your mouth or nose.
6. Appreciate the small pause before the next breath begins.

* * *

**Exercise 3: concentration breath—
helps to focus the mind**

1. **Begin as in exercise 2 to become aware of your breath.**
2. **As you breathe in, say to yourself "I am breathing in".**
3. **As the lungs deflate, say to yourself "I am breathing out".**

There is no need to change your breath for exercises 3 or 4 unless you want to slow it down or take it further into your belly. It can be used when you want to clear you mind of chatter or to stop yourself focusing on some pain or worry. It's a useful tool for bringing calm into potentially impatient moments such as traffic jams, queues and waiting rooms, or can be just a peaceful break from whatever you are doing.

**Exercise 4: mood-changing breath**

**As I've said elsewhere, it isn't always the best course of action to escape an emotion (working with and through it can have deeper and more lasting results), but there are times when we need to snap out of a feeling as soon as possible, such as when feeling afraid or**

**feeling some unhelpful tension arising. Then we can do the following exercise:**

1. **Notice and connect with your breathing and your body for a few breaths.**
2. **Then start to say to yourself as you breathe in "I breathe in calm".**
3. **And as you breathe out, say "I breathe out tension".**
4. **Continue this for as long as the circumstances allow or until your calm is restored.**

The qualities you are breathing in and out can be chosen to suit the occasion and what you say to yourself can be shortened such as:

- "**In confidence;out fear.**"
- **"In love; out anger."**
- **"In peace; out frustration."**
- **"In appreciation; out disappointment."**

There are still many more methods for using the breath as a helpful tool, and we will look at some of these later. For the moment, though, it is important that you practise these few as often as possible (and before moving on again) so that they come to mind instantly when a need arises. Please don't forget that this course is all about **putting into practice** these little life skills and proving to yourself that they work in a variety of situations.

# PROGRESS CHECK

So how is it going so far? If you are used to reading a book straight through to find what it has to offer, you may be struggling to control that urge. But, if you do that, you may take as long as I have to achieve the calm serenity that you could be experiencing from now for the rest of your life. My constant encouragement to you to practise, practise, practise before moving on is in order for you to have some more instant results.

So if, for a while now, you've been stopping and 'checking-in' throughout each day to notice where you are, what you're doing and how you're feeling, you could by now be noticing a special feeling that spreads through your body as you get in touch with it. I personally notice a relaxing and softening of my body, with a lovely wave of serenity that takes over my mind as well. It's a great feeling of well-being that usually causes me to break into a big smile. While I take my few deep breaths, I let the smile remain and let the energy of it spread through me.

If you're not achieving this state yet, don't worry; it will come, but it's easier for some than others. It's taken me years to get to this point because I haven't followed a structured practice to get there. That's why I'm presenting the method this way—so that others can take a shorter route to tranquillity. Once you get into the habit of creating this feeling for yourself, it should be a skill for life, giving you all the health benefits that a peaceful mind creates and helping you through any difficult patches in life.

What you might find, if you're anything like me, is that you can most easily remember to check in and feel the sense of calm on quiet days at home alone to start with, but forget all about it when with others or busy with some activity. You might even go complete days without giving the practice a thought. Then you might have a successful day with lots of practice or even several days when it comes easily. Eventually we want it to become a habit to check in frequently whatever is going on and, of course, the ultimate aim is to live in this centred, peaceful state all the time, unruffled by whatever life brings. A check-in at bedtime will tell you how peaceful you've felt that day and give you a chance to reset your resolve for tomorrow.

Before you move on, you need to be 'checking-in' on and off all day, every day, no matter what is going on, and hence be feeling waves of calm and well-being flowing through you. This will also mean that you are breathing more deeply and smiling a lot more frequently, both of which will be having therapeutic effects on your body. It might be a good idea at this stage to remind yourself of the many benefits this practice can bring you. And don't forget that, the more of a habit it becomes, the deeper and longer lasting will be the effects.

Some readers might well feel that they've learnt enough for now while some will be keen to learn more, and yet others may feel they need a lot longer to really master the process and gain any benefits. My suggestion is that you only move on if you are 'checking-in' regularly most days, even when there's a lot going on in your life, and if you are managing to notice and counteract a lot of the 'preventers'. Otherwise, I would suggest recapping what we've covered so far and giving yourself more time for practice. Maybe re-read from the start to check that you haven't forgotten anything or are missing something from your daily practice. This has often been my trouble through taking in too much at once. In any case, I recommend that you read just the next section to recap the benefits of this system and encourage you to persevere.

# THE BENEFITS OF 'CHECKING-IN' (OR WHY THIS PRACTICE IS REALLY WORTH DOING!)

We all know how pleasant it feels to completely relax, such as when we collapse into a cosy bed at the end of a tiring or trying day, or lie back in a comfy chair or on a warm beach and feel the warm sun on our skin. Well, there is no reason why we shouldn't achieve that feeling of total well-being far more often and more easily than most of us do. Scientists, by explaining what is going on in our bodies in response to our thoughts and actions, have given us good health reasons for watching those thoughts and becoming more aware of what is going on around and within us. When we stop the mind's constant rush and do the complete 'checking in' exercise, we are giving ourselves the following benefits:

1. Bringing to our notice tensions in the body so that we can let those tensions go.
2. Stopping the mind's constant chatter.

3. Halting the flow of the harmful stress chemicals such as cortisol around the body.
4. Promoting the release of endorphins—the beneficial chemicals.
5. Increasing oxygen intake to all our cells for optimum performance and to the brain for more clarity.
6. Lowering blood pressure.
7. Bringing our attention to the present moment, where we are experiencing life here and now and not an imaginary and maybe worrying future or a disturbing past that's gone forever.
8. Putting us back in control of our life by making us fully conscious.

# A NATURAL BREAK FOR MORE EXERCISES

Whether you are ready to move on or have chosen to recap the work so far, you might like to learn some more loosening exercises. I concentrate on loosening the body because we are trying to change old habits and rigid ways of thinking and, as you will shortly appreciate, I hope, attitudes of mind and body are inevitably linked. Becoming more physically flexible, which these exercises enable, leads us to a greater willingness to try new ways of thinking and being. The following 'opening' exercises not only help to open up the joints to allow the free flow of energy, but also open our thinking to new, helpful ideas. They have the additional benefit of improving blood flow to the joints to help keep them healthy. So, whether you already have your own routine of exercise or feel you get enough from walking, cycling, swimming, gym, etc., please make time to include some of the exercises in this programme as well.

I learnt the following set of exercises at a chi kung class years ago and use them almost every day, as they are designed to open and loosen all the main joints of the body. I realise that there will certainly be some readers who are unable to carry out some of these as they are a bit more demanding than the few we've covered so far. It is important with all new exercises that you do only those that you can manage safely and without pain. Please be very gentle with your body and exercise caution in what you attempt. Here's an idea!If you find any of these impossible or too painful, sit in a relaxed position, close your eyes, and visualise yourself carrying them out painlessly. This will be using the wonderful power of visualisation that sports people often use to improve their technique and achieve their goals, and which we will be looking into later.

**Exercise:**

**Stand with your feet hip-width apart, back as straight as possible and shoulders relaxed. Slowly and carefully work through the following joints. Hold on to something, if necessary, for those that require balancing on one leg.**

- **Ankles—in turn, put your weight on each leg and lift the other to rotate the foot a few times in each direction.**
- **Knees—with a hand on each knee, rotate them a few times in each direction (in towards each other and then away). Then put your knees together and rotate both a few times each way.**
- **Hips—(i) with your hands on your waist, rotate your pelvis a few times in each direction. (ii) with your arms out in front as if holding a large ball there, rotate each leg in a circle to the side, with the lower**

**leg hanging from the knee—a few times each leg.**

- **Waist—with hands still on your waist, bend your upper body towards one side, across the front and back up the other side a few times and then reverse the direction.**
- **Shoulders—make circles towards the back and then towards the front with either your shoulders only or by circling your arms.**
- **Elbows—lift both arms out in front of the body and rotate the lower arms a few times in each direction.**
- **Wrists—in the same way, rotate both hands a few times.**
- **Neck—very gently, moving the whole head, look from side to side a few times, then up and down, and finally round and round (there is usually a lot of scrunching noise with these, indicating how much tension the neck always holds, so you are not alone if you notice this!).**

# OUR BODY IS OUR BUDDY

You will have noticed how we can use our bodies to bring us away from our minds. By consciously bringing the focus of our attention down into our bodies, we stop some of the chatter and distraction that is going on in our heads. These days both our minds and bodies are given a lot of attention in the media, but not always for the most helpful reasons. Intellectual prowess;being a 'whizz kid' with computers; passing exams with flying colours; winning valuable general knowledge contests all bring admiration and are encouraged, as are many other feats requiring a concentration of brain power. The body, likewise, is praised and almost worshipped by some of society, not for the miraculous container that it is for our consciousness but for being slim, tanned, rippling with huge muscles, more attractive than others, etc. I 'm sure you understand what I mean.

I am certainly not saying that we shouldn't wonder at what can be achieved on the world stage by our minds and bodies. The human race has made amazing use of both to achieve incredible heights, with mind-boggling science taking us into space and repairing parts of the body that we can barely see. Sportsmen have exerted their bodies and minds to extremes in order to push ever outwards the barriers and limits so far achieved.

It's on the day-to-day level that I've discovered how valuable our body can be to us 'mere mortals' beyond moving us around and enabling us to carry out activities that are necessary or just pleasurable. It offers a brilliant feedback system that we very often simply ignore or just see as a nuisance because we've become 'top heavy' by being in our minds most of the time. We spend almost every waking second in our mind, turning our attention to the body only when it gives us trouble or when the mind tells us the body needs improving in some way. So even then we are imposing our will on the body, instead of appreciating and respecting it or listening to it with interest.

Its most obvious feedback is when something is wrong with the body itself and we get a message in the form of pain or other discomfort. This, of course, is its way of getting our attention so that we can do something about it. The neural network is sending impulses from the sensory nerves back to our brain for interpretation. Unfortunately, most of us only have limited ability to interpret exactly what is wrong, which is why we must visit a medical professional to help us pinpoint precisely what is the problem and what we need to do. I have a sneaky feeling that early man might have been better at diagnosing his own ailments, as can those now who are more in touch with their intuition (a subject for later on).

The feedback that is not so obvious is that which can tell us a lot about our emotions. This is how the body is our buddy in working our way towards more peace. Every emotion we experience is felt somewhere, if not everywhere, in the body. This makes it an invaluable friend in helping us with awareness.

There are some often-quoted examples to illustrate this, such as if you imagine eating something whose taste you dislike. It might make you instantly want to reject it, and your body may gag or heave. This is a thought having a physical effect on you, and also a sensation having a physical and emotional effect. When we experience the emotion of fear there are several ways in which the body reacts. We may notice our heart rate increasing, our palms sweating, a knotted feeling in our stomach/solar plexus area and additional symptoms according to the degree of fear felt. And, of course, sadness and happiness can bring tears to our eyes. These are all illustrations of how connected our minds, emotions and bodies are, and yet it is only comparatively recently that scientists have started to unravel the mechanisms behind this. It's a mixture of chemical and electrical systems and results in emotions being felt by every one of our trillions of cells. It also means that, if not dealt with skilfully, our emotions can settle into parts of our bodies and cause blockages in the energy flow, sometimes resulting in the compromised functioning of the affected part. I find particularly fascinating the many books that help to relate a particular physical disease or problem to some emotional cause. By understanding this we can use our minds as an additional tool in helping to heal ourselves.

Expressions such as 'he's a pain in the neck', 'she shoulders her family's problems', 'I can't handle this any more' can give us clues to the cause of problems and disease in the body parts concerned. It's an interesting line to study, some connections being more obvious than others, but often bringing us to a deeper understanding of what we are doing to ourselves. Take, for example, some of the following cases:I might develop a stiff neck if I'm with someone I find annoying and whom I consider 'a pain in the neck'. A chest infection might mean there's something I need to voice to someone—'get it off my chest', or I might develop a sore throat in such a circumstance. Hand problems could stem from being unable to let go of someone or something, while being 'weak at the knees' can indicate a fear of moving forward. There is proof of a connection between heart attacks and feeling broken-hearted, and those who feel stifled or smothered by others (sometimes by a parent) can develop breathing difficulties such as asthma.

This list goes on and on, and noticing the connections can be fascinating, enlightening and very helpful in getting to the root cause of physical ailments. The branch of science that covers this body/mind relationship is known as psychoneuroimmunology and I've found that a little understanding of some of it has been very helpful to myself and others with whom I've shared it. For the moment I have offered it for your consideration in order to stress the importance of including an awareness of your body in your breathing and 'here I am' exercises. It would be comparatively easy to just stop and take a few deep breaths now and then and this will calm the mind and bring us back to the present moment. However, the exercise is far more powerful when combined with getting in touch with our core self (the real me) and with the body. It gives the body a chance to release any tension and to offer its amazing feedback. So, I ask you to please develop the habit of always including a quick body scan with every 'checking in', 'here I am' interval.

**Exercise:**

**I'd like you just to try the following exercise in case it proves of any help to you. I realise it will appeal to some more than others:**

1. **Pick an ailment or problem that you currently have in your body.**
2. **In relation to that part of the body:**
   - **(i) think of a saying that refers to it, such as 'bending over backwards'.**
   - **(ii) think what that part represents (the back = support).**
   - **(iii) consider the functions of that part and whether any are not being fulfilled (an upright back enables us to stand up for ourselves).**
   - **(iv) look into whether this gives any insight into what thoughts or emotions could be behind the physical problem.**
   - **(v) take any remedial action that might be possible.**

## ACT AS IF (FURTHER USE OF THE MIND, EMOTION, BODY CONNECTION)

It can be interesting to observe how a person walks or holds himself, especially if you know anything about how they think or feel. A tendency to hollow the chest, for example, can indicate fear or feeling vulnerable or over-burdened, whereas an upright, purposeful walk probably indicates confidence or self-belief.

You might find it fun, as I do, to try different postures and walks in order to notice the feelings that result. This discovery can then be used to help create the way you want to feel, or even help relieve an adverse mind/body link. For example, walking upright and boldly in for an interview; smiling around a room full of strangers to counteract nervousness or shyness about doing that. You could imagine that, in a play, you are given the role of a person who feels the way you want to feel, and then try acting the way they would, physically. You might be surprised by the effect that has.

# UNDERSTANDING OUR CHEMICALS (AT A BASIC LEVEL, AT LEAST)

I'd like you to think back now to the exercise we did involving the two traffic jam scenarios. Remember that when you were fighting reality and wishing you had taken a different route, worrying about being late for the appointment and anxiously watching the traffic queue ahead, you noticed tension building and felt uncomfortable in your body as well as in your mind. Then you did the 'checking in' exercise, relaxed your body with some deep breaths and started to look around with interest, accepting what was happening. You noticed how much pleasanter this felt. Let's look now at how I understand this actually happens.

My knowledge of this aspect of science is very much a lay-person's and there are plenty of books to give more detailed and scientific descriptions for those that are interested. I really enjoyed William Bloom's *The Endorphin Effect* and *Molecules of Emotion* by Candace Pert, PhD, the former of these having enabled me to take a big leap forward in learning to restore calm in stressful times. I hope that the following understanding will, at least, be enough to encourage you to do the exercises.

When we have any thought, the body automatically sets in motion a chain of actions that involves electrical impulses and the release of chemical messengers throughout the body. The purpose of this instant transmission of information is to prepare the body for action, and sometimes this is vital, such as in the case of imminent danger. In the face of a serious threat, the body has to stop some functions, such as digestion, and direct all its energy to life-preserving strategies such as being able to run for its life or fight off an attacker (the flight or fight response). Every cell knows about the thought and is affected by the chemicals related to it. Some of the rational thinking part of the brain even cuts out in panic mode.

All these natural reactions happen to some extent however slight the negative feeling. Just a fleeting thought about something unpleasant will trigger the message-sending system. We can be aware of the effects in the body as when our stomach feels knotted or fluttery, our heart rate increases, our palms begin to sweat, or our breathing is affected. The strength of these sensations depends on the degree of fear, anxiety, embarrassment, resistance, etc. that we are experiencing and, with awareness, we can notice the body telling us that we are in stress mode.

The two best known stress chemicals are cortisol and adrenalin, both of which are essential to the normal healthy functioning of our bodies. Of course, we recognise adrenalin as the one that stimulates action such as in the flight or fight situation. I'm not advocating that we resist it at all costs because it is there for a reason. We obviously need it for competitive activities and dare-devil thrills (if we feel inclined towards those!), and it plays its part in enthusiasm, excitement, and courage, as well as general bodily functions. What we do want to avoid is switching on these stress signals too often and unnecessarily, especially with no immediate physical release of the stress, causing interruptions to the healthy harmony within our bodies. We obviously can't avoid these vital chemical releases altogether, but we can limit their release to essential times by giving up the mental habits that create them, such as excessive worrying, fighting reality or frightening ourselves with imagined scenarios.

On the other hand, there are 'friendly' chemicals that we want to encourage, and the good news is that we can learn how to stimulate the release of these at will and thus benefit from their mood- and health-enhancing effects. There is serotonin, responsible for sensations of pleasure, and oxytocin nicknamed the 'kindness hormone' for the part it plays in kind and altruistic acts and thoughts. It is also instrumental in the bonding between mothers and babies. The group that I have found most useful to learn about and use, and the one we are going to look into and use here, is the endorphin group. They are part of the neuropeptide family of which there are about 100 and include our DNA. They are produced in the brain and throughout the body and carry information around to all our cells. They can be thought of as the body's version of morphine as their effects are so similar. Here are some of the things that endorphins can do for us by softening tissue to allow the better flow of energy.

They can:

- reduce or kill pain
- counteract stress
- create feelings of pleasure (from tastes, sights, memories)

- help healing
- boost immunity
- create bliss states (as in meditation)
- release tension
- allow absorption of universal energy.

Endorphins make us feel good and we can stimulate their release by thinking. Isn't that wonderful news? In fact, when we do our 'checking in' exercise, completely relax into our body and come back to a calm and peaceful way of being that is exactly what we are doing. We are releasing endorphins into our blood stream and immune system. It's a two-way flow. Endorphins make us feel good and feeling good releases endorphins. So, we can now use this knowledge to bring about any of the above benefits as and when we feel the need, or simply use it to enhance how we feel minute by minute throughout our lives. Even better news is that, in addition to the 'checking in' exercise and deep breathing, we can cause the release of endorphins just by thinking of something positive—something that makes us feel good, and even by the physical act of smiling.

**Exercise 1:**

**I suggest you set aside at least 15 minutes for this exercise. In your journal or on a large clean sheet of paper write the heading *smileys*, and list some of your favourite things. These will be things that give you a warm feeling inside, bring a smile to your face, make you chuckle or some other pleasant sensa-**

**tion (such as making your mouth water in the case of a favourite taste), and you began this list way back at the start of this guide. They might include events, people, places, animals, tastes, colours, smells, experiences, or activities that bring you a 'smiley' feeling. Don't include, though, any memories that also bring regrets as these would have a negating effect on the exercise. Keep the list positive.**

Just doing this exercise will have been beneficial to you however many 'smileys' you have on your list, and I hope you have noticed a change in your mood for the better. I'd like you to keep the list handy and add to it as you think of more things. You might find that you now begin to notice more things that have a good effect on you. Make sure you add them to the list.

**Exercise 2:**

1. **Sit in a relaxed position and choose one item from your list, picking one that gives you a strong happy feeling.**
2. **Close your eyes and visualise the person, place, or event with as many of your senses as possible.**

**For example, one of my favourites is a bluebell wood, so I visualise myself sitting on a**

**log surrounded by bluebells with a sea of them stretching in all directions around me. I hear the birds in the wood singing, smell the flowers' delicate scent and feel the warm sun coming through the pale green leaves. (The ability to visualise improves with practice so don't give up if you don't feel very able to do this at first—keep trying.)**

3. **Stay with your visualisation for several minutes and then notice how you feel.**

* * *

**Exercise 3:**

**I suggest now that you leave your list, and cease reading for a time while you get on with something else that you have to do. As you get on with whatever this is, I hope you will be aware of where your thoughts are taking you. In each of your 'checking-in' moments during this time, turn your attention to one of your 'smileys' and notice the difference it makes to your feeling, and how much easier it is then to add an inner or a physical smile to the exercise.**

* * *

**Exercise 4:**

**Sitting in a relaxed position now, bring to mind one of your favourite 'smileys' and really sink into the good feeling it brings. Now, see if you can visualise this feeling spreading throughout your body or going to an area that is feeling pain, discomfort, or particular tension. Let the feeling rest there and see if the area softens and relaxes more.**

By directing the feeling to a part of the body we can concentrate the endorphins there to do their healing and restorative work.

Apart from using this technique in each 'checking in' session, it can be very beneficial to bring 'smileys' to mind at the following times:

- when feeling unhappy about something
- when in pain or discomfort
- when feeling tired or overwhelmed
- before a challenge
- at waiting times such as traffic lights, queues, train journeys
- in bed when sleep won't come
- when you have to endure something you don't like, such as an unpleasant medical treatment or a frustrating business meeting
- as often as possible for holistic well-being.

On this same theme, it is worth looking into what we have around us that we enjoy (pictures, etc.) and what we do on a regular basis. Now that we know we can enhance our health and well-being in this way, it is important to make more space and time for 'smileys' in our everyday lives. Thinking of something you've enjoyed during the day can help to calm and uplift you before sleep, setting endorphins to work in that valuable state.

# THE MAGICAL ACT OF SMILING

## TWO USEFUL FACTS THAT I'VE LEARNT ALONG LIFE'S PATH

**Frowning uses far more face muscles and energy than smiling does.**

**Smiling creates endorphins in the body—those life-enhancing chemicals (*whether you mean the smile or not*).**

So, as we swap our negative thoughts for positive ones, why not smile at the same time? Isn't it amazing that so much is spent on various pills and supplements that claim to help us stay upbeat and healthy while all we need to do is turn on our own smiles? Another wonderful benefit, of course, is that our smile can lift another's spirit by releasing their endorphins too. A smile can be like a germ in its ability to spread, but one that we can be proud to pass on to others. Just imagine, if we started an epidemic of smiling, how great that could feel. It might well develop into a full-blown case of giggles or belly laughter, with all their attendant symptoms and side-effects!

Of course, we all have times when we feel we have absolutely nothing to smile about. I notice the pain in someone's eyes sometimes when they obviously can't bring themselves to return a smile, and I have had painful occasions myself when I know I would normally smile at someone or about something but I can't drag myself up out of the mire of despair I've let myself sink into.

Then I learnt about the magic of the smile so that this very rarely happens to me now and, if I do catch myself (through awareness) slipping into that hopeless state of mind, I can grab myself back out of it and gradually bring my spirits back up at least to a more peaceful state, where I can properly feel and deal with the feelings that have taken me there.

First of all, I remind myself of the scientific evidence that smiling releases endorphins into my system. Just as I don't want to feed my body something that makes it ill (tuna makes me as sick as a dog), neither do I want to send stress hormones coursing through my system. It makes obvious sense to flood myself with endorphins, *especially* when I am feeling low. There doesn't even have to be a happy feeling behind the smile. Isn't that amazing? The subconscious that, let's face it, is very easily fooled, responds to the physical action of smiling anyway.

And this is where another previously mentioned discovery comes in: that, if we 'act as if' we feel a certain way for long and consistently enough, we will actually begin to feel that way. Yes, I found that one a hard fact to swallow and there is only one way to test it of course. I do hope you can believe me on this one as it really does work and can also be extremely valuable in building self-esteem. Maybe a personal example will help you to see its uses and, incidentally, remind you that I am just another learner like yourself, still catching myself now and then slipping back into old ways through losing my awareness. There are always challenges to test us and hopefully, as you get more practised with all these tricks, you will actually come to enjoy some of the opportunities to see how you're progressing.

Anyway, a short while ago I let myself get very down in the dumps over what was looking like a lost friendship. Someone I had got to know over a few months and whose company I had really enjoyed and appreciated suddenly disappeared out of my life with no explanation. I was aware of my mind trying to torment me with thoughts such as 'what if...' and 'was it something I did or said?', 'if only...', which I managed to spot and banish most of the time by coming back to the present moment. One day my impatience and frustration took me into a real sadness, and I couldn't even enjoy the beautiful autumn colours through which I was driving. I was horrified when I noticed this fight I was having with reality and realised the harm that these feelings were doing me.

First of all I decided to spend some time just feeling fully each emotion, one by one (another technique we will be covering), and then I remembered to smile anyway at and in appreciation of nature's fabulous autumn show. I knew that such a display would normally bring me great joy, so I smiled as if I were feeling that joy. I kept the smile on my face as I drove on and a short time later found I was smiling at myself for getting into such a state. The smile I forced had seriously calmed my thoughts and emotions and lifted me to a state of mind where I could get everything back in proportion. In this case I came from obsession and devastation to the milder emotion of disappointment and then acceptance, with a willingness to let the matter go. I could actually feel a wave of relief and calm flow through my body, which I recognised as the flow of those feel-good chemicals flooding every cell.

So now, guess what!I am suggesting that you practise the act of smiling so much that it really becomes a habit. Some readers, of course, might have noticed already the contribution smiling makes to the calm and peaceful state reached by 'checking-in' and breathing in the 'here I am' exercises. If you don't already add a smile to your check-ins, please do so from now on a regular basis and, as often as possible, practise the following exercises until they too become a habit.

**Exercise 1:**

**When you open the curtains or blinds in the morning, or you first look out of the window, smile at the day, whether, in your opinion, the weather is good or bad.**

* * *

**Exercise 2:**

**Every time you catch sight of yourself in a mirror, stop and smile at yourself. This has the added benefit of boosting self-esteem.**

**Even if you don't like something about the image you see there, make yourself give a polite and kindly smile, or, better still if you can, a loving one.**

* * *

**Exercise 3:**

**Smile in as many of the following situations as you can:**

- **when you change a negative thought to a positive one**
- **before you make a phone call, write an email, letter, or text, smile as if to the person you are addressing, even if you don't know them or don't actually like them**
- **writing greeting cards and wrapping presents**
- **to people whose eyes you meet in passing**

## THE INNER SMILE

Finally, on the smile theme, I'd like to introduce the Inner Smile, about which I've read in several places and the practising of which I know has been found to be very therapeutic. It also fits wonderfully into my philosophy of creating a harmonious relationship between body, mind and spirit.

**Exercise 4:**

1. **Think of one of your list of 'smileys' until you feel the smiley feeling inside.**
2. **Notice where this feeling is in your body.**
3. **Visualise it spreading into every part of your body, and every cell smiling. Stay with this feeling for as long as you like.**

## REMINDERS

**Before you move on to the next section, please spend some time revising what you've learnt and carrying out the following practices:**

1. Make time for some loosening exercises every day, even if it's only five minutes in the morning.
2. Regularly stop to 'check-in' to how your body feels, and release tensions with some deep breaths, a smile and remembering some of your 'smileys'.
3. When your mind gets too busy, notice where it's gone and use the appropriate 'cure' to bring you back to the present moment.
4. Give some thought to any physical pain or discomfort, looking for what thoughts and emotions could be behind it.

5. Smile as often as possible and smile to your body.
6. Don't forget to belly-breathe. It needs lots of practice. And do some mood-changing breaths when you need to.
7. Keep adding 'smileys' to your list and think about them often, especially during difficult times.

# KNOWING WHEN TO STOP

By now I hope your days are interspersed with little intervals of 'checking-in'—coming back into your body from your busy mind, taking a few deep breaths and feeling gratitude for something that's in your life or in your immediate surroundings and, of course, smiling. This can be likened to taking a small dose of elixir for the benefit of your health. Mind, body and spirit all benefit from these islands of tranquillity, as they send healing endorphins flowing through your system.

Even with this practice firmly established in my life I still find, occasionally, that my whole being longs for a complete relaxation. It needs more than is achieved by watching television, reading, walking, or chatting with friends. There are some days when I just don't want to do anything and maybe even stay in bed. You may or may not recognise this feeling. Of course, it's rarely possible to simply give in to it, but I do notice it and promise myself some time off in the very near future. There is usually a good reason for feeling like this, which may be that my body is fighting off some germs or that my mind has been overloaded with too much thinking. It might simply be that I've been overdoing everything—maybe even having too much fun!

To achieve the time off might mean altering plans, postponing some jobs or some socialising. It might also entail having to say 'no' to people, duties, or activities and this is something else we need to learn to be able to do in a kind but firm way. The time off does need to be given some priority, however, otherwise I've noticed that I get sick with a bad cold or some other affliction so that I end up having no choice but to put off everything else. Another consequence of battling on despite the warning signs can be that our temperament becomes more negative, maybe snapping at others and generally not being the peaceful, amiable people we want to be.

Most of us have great difficulty with allowing ourselves to completely relax. We are conditioned not to be lazy, not to skive, not to procrastinate, etc. so even when we try to take time off, we have a little voice of guilt nagging away at us or a busy bit of our mind reminding us of what still needs to be done.

On the other hand, we might be choosing to stay busy all the time because we know that stopping leaves us free to face some uncomfortable feelings such as loneliness or grief. These feelings rarely go away on their own so it would be better for us to acknowledge and then spend some time with the emotions, working through them, with help if necessary. Then we will be free to totally relax mind and body.

Some people have an underlying fear that they might sound boring to their friends and family if they admit to spending some time just being, or doing nothing. They prefer to have a list of activities to report when they speak to them, or even get caught up in a subconscious competition for who has the busiest and (in their belief) the most interesting life. If you do have difficulty on this score, it might be worth considering what it is that causes you to resist the idea of stopping.

To achieve the best relaxation we can, we need to connect mind and body. Escaping into a good book or film, or interacting with others in however pleasurable a way that may be, still keeps the mind busy and possibly creates tension in the body. We need to find a method to free our whole being for a certain period until we feel the energy and enthusiasm coming back, indicating that our cells have recovered their harmony and are restored sufficiently to support us in a healthy state.

Part of the method I use is to 'let the day take over', or 'go with the flow', so I decide to have no 'should' for the day and no jobs that must be done. I also have to ban any thought about the jobs that will still be waiting after my time off, because worrying about jobs can be even more stressful than doing them might be. I make being in the present moment and connected to my body a priority, allowing time to be with any feelings that are around, such as guilt, impatience, frustration, confusion, tiredness—noticing them, feeling them and letting them go.

These days, a decision will also have to be made about our electronic social connections, and will depend on our individual feelings about whether allowing these will be relaxing or not. You may find it easier to achieve by getting away from people and familiar surroundings in order to avoid the reminders and distractions—maybe just out in nature somewhere—or to stay in one room or in bed between mealtimes in order to remain focused within. If sleep comes, that's OK and obviously what the body needs. Sometimes this need for total relaxation can be caused by the immune system fighting off some invader, or by one of our organs feeling overloaded and needing time to heal. Extra sleep provides the time and space for our bodies to do just that. On awaking, remember to reconnect mind and body, and notice the feelings that are there.

During this time off there will arise ideas or impulses to do something, as most of us are so averse to just being. Notice these urges and the resistance to being idle and, if you are really struggling, try to restrict yourself to some very simple activities with some 'down' time in between. I sometimes do some writing about how I'm feeling, go for a slow, gentle stroll, noticing as much as I can along the way (i.e. being very mindful), listen to some calming music, all the while staying as aware as possible of what is happening, within and without. Words such as lazy and idle may creep up on you now and then during this time, especially if you have to tell anyone else (an unexpected visitor, partner, etc.) what you are (not) doing. Simply counteract these thoughts each time by replacing them with words such as healing, restoring, connecting, recharging my batteries, chilling out, having some 'me' time, or just relaxing. Don't forget that we are human *beings*, not human *doings*.

It may be that the sitting still is the most challenging aspect, in which case I find myself doing the odd little menial task like a bit of dusting, re-arranging a cupboard, sorting some papers, or a little garden pottering. One important thing is that these activities are not planned or on 'the list' (of jobs), and the urge to do them arises spontaneously. The other important factor is that they are carried out mindfully, still very aware of my senses and feelings. I tend to avoid the computer, television, radio and even books as too distracting and too familiar in everyday life. These 'stopping' periods have to be different and have a different feel to them so that they can bring about their therapeutic results. An alternative way to make the time different is to get absorbed in something creative for which you usually feel you haven't the time, such as painting, writing poems, playing an instrument, or doing a creative craft.

It may occur to you to wonder how this sort of day is better than just doing something you love. Well, I've recently had one of each sort of day. On one day I went off to the beach to swim, read a novel, lie on the sand, have a picnic, swim again and eventually return after six hours, feeling great. My mind and, to some extent, my body had rested. On the other day, I was not inclined to do anything physical or mental so realised that my whole being needed more of a break. I chose to stay at home, being mindful, and doing very little. I felt my energy and enthusiasm gradually restore as the day progressed. Being in touch with my body and aware of its feedback made it possible for me to notice what it really needed in each case. In the second one my body, mind and spirit all called for an empty sort of rest, and all three benefitted from it.

I realise that, being retired, I have the privilege of more free time than many readers but I used to practise this when I was still working, for at least a few hours now and then. It's an investment of time that pays back dividends in the form of more energy, efficiency, health, and calm well-being. It might be that you notice a need for some quiet time, especially after being with people a lot. We pick up others' energies and sometimes we need to 'detox' ourselves back to our calm centre. These periods, however long they need to be, will lead to feeling lighter, freer, and more energetic, which somehow makes tackling everyday chores and duties much more pleasurable.

This means that, far from it being a waste of time, as some may see it, *being* time actually leads to more productivity in the long run—and certainly better health. I do hope you will give it a try.

**STOPPING RECAP**

**Be alone if possible, by saying "No" to distracting people or activities. Think of the time as healing mind and body tiredness or overload. Resist television, books, talking radio and social media. Forget your list of jobs. If necessary, get away from familiar surroundings that will remind you of 'the list', chores, etc. Sleep if necessary, or stay as aware as possible of internal feelings and your surroundings. Keep coming back to your breath and body. Smile frequently. Swap any negative thoughts for positives, e.g. gratitude, favourite things (smileys). Keep appreciating the time off you are giving yourself—wallowing in the luxury of it if you like!**

## HIBERNATION

Don't worry, I'm not going to suggest that you build up a big layer of body fat, dig a burrow and go to sleep for the winter! But I have found that changing my attitude to, and my leisure activities during, the winter months has had a very positive effect on my peace of mind during the darker, colder half of the year.

I know some people have no trouble at all with the shortening days, dropping temperatures and falling leaves and then snow, but I do meet more people of the opposite persuasion, who bemoan all of these happenings. Many of them even become miserable and depressed from the moment the clocks go back until the warmth and signs of new life return with the spring. I have one friend who starts to dread the winter as soon as we reach the summer solstice in late June, seeing it as all downhill until Christmas, despite there being a lot of summer left—an excellent example of how our thoughts can cause us grief!

I know there are those who actually suffer from SAD (Seasonal Affective Disorder), which may be related to their hormone/chemical make-up, and you have my sympathy. Hopefully you are aware of remedies such as the sunshine lamps available to help with this. I do wonder, though, whether you might still be able to lift your spirits by practising the acceptance and adaptations that have worked for me.

To some extent it depends on your constitution and physical make-up as to which season suits you best. I have always felt my healthiest and most energetic during the spring and summer and used not to be able to understand those who said they loved the autumn for more than its show of glorious colour. I still hugely prefer the warmer months, not only for their warmth that I love, but also for the extra activities we can get up to and the way nature blossoms with so much vigour and colour. So, I have to admit that I used to tend to be pretty negative about the autumn and winter months until I realised I could choose a different way to think about it. Remember, we can always change our thoughts!

I decided to stop depressing myself with my resistance and looked around at the way the rest of nature (of which I'm a part) behaves. At the latitudes of the Earth that experience this change in seasons, a lot of nature closes down and rests for the period when we move away from the sun, so maybe we human animals could benefit from a quieter time as well. Just as we need some sleep in every 24 hours, maybe we need some time to slow down, withdraw and rest to some extent on a larger scale than just the odd day off. Unfortunately, because of the way our society works, I realise that it isn't possible for the majority to give up their means of earning a living. Neither do I suggest that we should all stay indoors as much as possible, because we need the health-giving fresh air and exercise.

So, what has helped me to make the most of winter? **Choice**. I decided to look forward to the less distracting months (I find it very hard to stay indoors when the sun's shining!) to catch up with jobs and activities that I never seem to have time for in the spring and summer. I still carry on as normal on some days and get plenty of exercise and social contact, but I also actually look forward to long evenings and bad weather days to do some 'inner' work. In fact, I now make a list during the year of 'winter jobs' so that, by the time summer comes to an end, I'm actually looking forward to getting on with the list, such as decluttering, repairs and renewals around the house or a creative hobby, plus guiltlessly allowing myself to hibernate a bit with books and films I never have time for during my active months.

It is also true of course that there are probably people who feel just the opposite. Those who don't look forward to and don't function well during hot weather might well tend towards hibernation during the summer months by staying indoors and catching up with the activities they don't have time for when the seasons change, and they are out and about pursuing autumn and winter activities. Although they don't have the natural cycle of nature on their side, it is best for them to listen to their own bodies and adjust accordingly.

Although I am sure readers can think up their own list of examples, here are a few suggestions for the kind of things you might consider for a hibernation period of whatever length and at whatever time you feel is best for you:

- **Sort and possibly de-clutter possessions and paperwork.**
- **Do some deep-cleaning or decorating at home.**
- **Take up a new hobby.**
- **Spend time on a creative activity.**
- **Catch up with some reading or film watching, that you don't usually have time for.**
- **Spend more time just being or listening attentively to favourite music.**
- **Learn and practise some new recipes.**
- **Give your body a health-holiday, detox or book some pampering treatments.**

**Of course, another choice is available and preferred by some who prefer to avoid the change of seasons altogether by travelling elsewhere in the world!**

Apart from seasonal changes that we can prepare for physically and mentally, we may have unexpected changes thrust upon us in life, totally out of the blue. I'm thinking here of accidents, illness, lifestyle changes, big emotional upsets, and others, all of which can cause us to give up our usual activities and way of life. We could call them 'fallow' periods and, because we can't continue life at the same pace for physical or emotional reasons, we may find ourselves forced into a kind of hibernation of inactivity. This is when it can be so helpful to remember that we are human **beings** and that we have an inner world that can benefit from periods of reflection and regeneration. The important point to remember regarding all of these occasions (just like everything else) is that we have a **choice** how to feel about anything and, if we find something we can't change is causing us some negative emotion, then we have to **accept it** first and, if possible, **change our attitude** to it in order to **stay calm and peaceful.**

# GRATITUDE AND APPRECIATION— TWO GREAT HELPERS

The meanings of these two words and the emotions they represent are so similar that I'm never sure which one I am feeling. Being grateful is more often used when receiving something or in relation to something for which we are thankful. Appreciation can be used in the same context but can also have the wider meaning of seeing the beauty in something or someone. But don't let us worry about these subtleties here. My general meaning and the emotion I want us to work on is thankfulness, for which I may use either word.

If you look back at your list of 'smileys', I'm sure you'll find that many of them are there because you are grateful for them or for the ability to enjoy them. Because we know that these 'smileys' are good for us to think about, it follows that an attitude of gratitude must also be worth cultivating. It might encourage you to know that, in my quest to find and practise tools to enable me to feel good, cultivating a grateful frame of mind has been one of the easier ones. However despairing I may feel at any time, I have to say that I never fail to find something in my life to appreciate, when I remember to do so, and this lifts my spirit.

When things go 'wrong' in our lives—in other words, when we wish circumstances were different from how they are—our spirit sags and we feel flat or sad at best (until we stop fighting reality). At worst, we become enraged, desolate or even out of control. We call all of these emotions 'negative' and would prefer not to feel them. Life inevitably brings along, from time to time, events and circumstances that trigger the thoughts that cause these emotions. Most would agree that an ability to lessen these feelings and return to a 'positive' emotional state is well worth learning. By the way, I'm putting inverted commas around negative and positive because, in an ideal state of total acceptance of things as they are, nothing is good or bad. Well, I haven't got to that stage yet. I don't know about you!)

Hopefully, you have already been practising the 'smiley' exercises, physical smiling and having a go at 'acting as if' when you want to get into a better frame of mind, and I hope you are remembering these at appropriate times and finding them helpful. Well, here's how the gratitude helper works.

No matter how low, desperate, angry, or fearful you feel, you make yourself think of something for which to be grateful. Just managing to remember one thing is a start and cannot fail to lift your spirit, however slightly, while you consider it. If you can manage more, the more lifted you will feel, and the better you focus on your appreciation, the greater the effect will be.

I hear the protest: "Supposing everything's wrong with my life and there's nothing to appreciate?" Without wishing to sound unsympathetic, I have to point out that everyone should be able to find something, however small, to be grateful for. Even hostages and prisoners have been known to describe how they endured incredibly lengthy and difficult ordeals by focusing on something that they appreciated. For most everyday upsets we can be thankful for something like our health, fitness, a good night's sleep, a relationship we treasure, where we live, even our sanity and ability to think and reason. Some might appreciate what nature has to offer—warm sun, fresh water, birdsong, the reliability of the sunrise, the lack of storm or flood.

Bigger traumas will obviously need more effort. The deeper we fall into our negativity, the harder it may be to climb out, but everyone still has something to appreciate. For instance, everyone reading this could be grateful for the ability to read; for their eyesight; the huge fund of help that's out there on the bookshelves and internet; for someone who loves them; or for a happy memory. As a last resort, when it feels impossible to get into an appreciative frame of mind, how about thinking about how things could be worse or of what others are suffering? No-one is suffering every possible hardship at once, so there must be many bad experiences out there that we're not getting at present: let's be thankful for that fact. I must stress that I would use this only as a very last resort as it feels a bit uncomfortable to make myself feel better through another's worse circumstances and, if using this thought, I would also take the opportunity to have compassion for their plight.

The point is that the mere act of appreciation of anything moves our vibration or mood in an upward direction. It's like changing gear from reverse to forward, which moves us from negative to positive, from dark towards light, maybe even by only a tiny step, but it is the right direction. The tiny step makes a lot of difference and each appreciation can be seen as a rung on the ladder, up which we will climb out of our pit of despair.

## THE GRATITUDE HABIT

So far I've only talked about using these two helpers in emergencies, when we need rescuing from a negative frame of mind we've let ourselves slide into. Of course, this will happen less often as we become more aware of where our thoughts are taking us and better at using all the tools we've learnt to avoid this happening. In fact, you might be there already. Whether you are managing to stay calm and peaceful most of the time or not, I encourage you now to uplift your mood still further on a regular basis and to benefit your health even more by using gratitude as often as possible. I started with exercises like the following and now find myself reflecting on things to be grateful for on and off all the time, with extra big sessions of appreciation when I feel like a boost.

Let's not forget also to feel positive emotions as much as we can while we are experiencing them. I've talked a lot about stopping ourselves and 'checking-in' in order to bring our thoughts back from causing uncomfortable feelings, and the opposite of this is to stop and dwell on good thoughts that we are having. Let's remember to stop and 'check-in' to the joy and contentment of happy times and pleasurable sensations when they are with us. The more we can do this, the better it is for our mind, body and spirit.

**Exercise 1:**

**Every morning or last thing at night, list in your journal five things for which you are grateful. Either keep the same five things for a few days or a week at a time or find five new ones every day. They can be as basic as you like, such as having a roof over your head or a bed to sleep in, and this might help you get started.**

* * *

**Exercise 2:**

**Start to appreciate familiar things in your everyday life as you notice or use them, such as things about your home, your family, your friends, helpful appliances, etc. For example, feel grateful for the warm water when you use it; for the ability to contact distant friends or family;for comfortable furniture to relax into; the ability to travel around.**

* * *

**Exercise 3:**

**When you have to do a task for which you are feeling resistance such as cleaning the kitchen floor, for example, be grateful for aspects of the job. These might simply be the facts that you have a kitchen at all; that you have clean water, detergent, and tools to make the job easier; that you are physically able to carry out the job. Once again, an attitude of gratitude moves us from negative thinking and in this case might enable us to even enjoy otherwise unattractive chores.**

# 'SMILEY' PLUS— AN NLP TECHNIQUE

NLP stands for Neurolinguistic Programming and is a therapy that can be used to overcome fears and phobias and help deal with difficult situations by bringing about a change in the patient's emotions. There is a lot one can learn under this heading, but I am covering here just one technique that I have sometimes used successfully and which I know others have found helpful.

I actually touched on the process used in this science when I described how we have to create new neural pathways in the brain when the old, learned habits, beliefs, thoughts and actions no longer serve us. Remember how I likened the technique to destroying the old motorways and improving and enlarging the country lanes until they become the routes that our reactions automatically choose. We have so far been achieving this by watching our thoughts and learning which thought patterns to avoid or correct so that, instead of being led by our mind into discomfort and stress, we restore our equanimity and stay calm and peaceful more of the time.

An NLP practitioner would explain the science and the techniques that can be used and should then give the client some practice with the different techniques, possibly designing them to suit the particular issue that is bothering them. The technique we are covering here is for general use and fits nicely with the work we've done so far, as we can use one of our favourite 'smileys' and make use of the body/mind connection that I hope by now is understood and accepted by all readers. It is a way of using this connection in order to make the 'smiley' action quicker to work and even more powerful.

## THE METHOD

**Try this as an exercise**

1. **Pick a favourite 'smiley' from your list—one that reliably gives you a really calm feeling and brings you out of any uncomfortable or stressful feeling.**
2. **Decide on a small physical action that you can do inconspicuously that you would be able to do in most circumstances—something that others shouldn't notice you doing. We'll call this the 'trigger'. Some examples that students have come up with are:**
   - **squeezing a thumb with the opposite hand**
   - **tucking a thumb into the curled fingers of its hand**

- **pressing hard on any part of a hand**
- **pushing a fingernail gently into a finger**
- **pressing both thumbs together**
- **interlacing the fingers on both hands and putting some pressure on the knuckles.**

3. **Having decided on your 'smiley' and your 'trigger', concentrate on your 'smiley' until you are feeling your best—with that beautiful, relaxed, calm and peaceful feeling inside.**
4. **Now operate your 'trigger' while you are in that state and hold it for several seconds.**

This method works by association so that, with *lots of practice*, your brain messages will choose the new neural pathway (to create tranquillity in any circumstances) as soon as you use your 'trigger', without you even having to think about your 'smiley'. However, *it will need lots of practice* to establish the connection. I suggest a few minutes' practice every day, getting really into your smiley feeling, until the trigger works reliably. Still, think of all the good feelings and health benefits you'll be having while you are doing the practising!Then all you have to do is remember to use it!

# COME UP FOR AIR—PROGRESS CHECK WITH A BIT OF REVISION

Well, we've covered a lot of ground since your last progress check and break. I think it would be good now for you to stop reading any further for a while, unless of course you are managing to remember everything you've read and are using it all successfully already. In which case, many congratulations but maybe you could still do with a break to consolidate everything. When I'm learning something new, and especially when I have to remember to use what I've learnt, I like to test myself sometimes and do some extra practice with anything that has slipped through my memory net. (And there's bound be something!)

So, here's a suggested plan and some questions for testing and revising what you should be remembering to use on a regular basis by now:

1. **First of all, look back at the two sections on breathing ('Stop and breathe' and 'A bit more breathing'). Recap any techniques that you've not been using by**

**trying them out again. Notice which of all the types of breathing work best for you and resolve to make time every day to practise them.**

2. **Let's recap the 'full works' for the 'checking in' process.**
3. **At frequent intervals throughout the day, you should now be stopping, taking some deep breaths, coming back into your body/centre, noticing any tension in your body, what you are doing and where your thoughts have gone. If necessary, you should take remedial action by using the appropriate 'cure'. Then you can complete the exercise by looking around and appreciating your surroundings or something in them, smiling and/or thinking of a 'smiley' until you feel your calm and peaceful self returning. You can then go back to what you were doing in this improved state. If you've been very absorbed in something or been still for quite a while, get up and move, and look around for a few moments, shaking any parts of your body that feel stiff.**
4. **If you are not 'checking in' as often as you would like, do you need to create more reminders such as sticky notes around the home or office, or reminders on your phone?**
5. **Can you list the six general 'preventers' and remember a quick 'cure' for each one? If not, please refresh your memory by re-reading that section as it's an important one.**
6. **I suggest you re-read your 'smiley' list and see if you can add some more items. Read it slowly, visualising each item, so that you benefit from their effect.**

7. **Have you developed any aches or pains lately? If so, can you see any possible connection with well-known sayings about that part of the anatomy and could that shed some light on how your thinking may have a bearing on the problem and could be used to help alleviate it?**
8. **Are you still doing your daily gratitudes? If not, please try to get back into the habit.**
9. **If you haven't succeeded with creating an NLP trigger yet, keep working at it, and, if you have a working one now, are you remembering to use it in challenging circumstances such as during confrontations, patience-testing times, unpleasant or worrying situations (dentist/interview, etc.)?**

# SELF-ESTEEM (PART 1)

The degree of our inner peace depends hugely on our self-esteem, and this often showed up in the groups I worked with as a cause of some of the stress. It influences how we feel about events and circumstances in our lives. It colours our relationships with other people by affecting our reactions to them and how we regard them. A problem with this is that our self-esteem is created by our experiences from the moment we're born, allowing us no control over it in the early, most formative years. If we are rejected, even as a baby or small child, this registers in our consciousness and leads us to thinking that we are pretty worthless or unimportant. As babies, we arrive believing that we are the centre of the universe and are capable of anything, but this gets eroded as we grow up. Children are very attuned to people's reactions to, and feelings for, them, and their brains are coming to conclusions about all of this and storing it into their make-up. It shows up then in our personality because beliefs lodge in our subconscious whether they are true or not. Then these beliefs surface later, prompted by a current event.

And it doesn't stop at childhood. Teenage years can have even more effect as we try to establish where we fit in the hierarchy of our family and friends. At this stage, physical appearance also becomes an important issue. Our parents have expectations of us that we can't always live up to, and the world might feel like a competitive jungle with only the fittest 'surviving' in the popular sense of the word, which can mean a variety of things from having lots of friends or being top of the class to becoming a superstar or amassing a fortune. If our self-esteem has been taking blows all our life, we begin to feel like the weaklings in this jungle—of little importance or even rubbish in the eyes of the world, which is always an inaccurate self-assessment.

This is pretty bad news, and sadly applies to many people today. Those who become addicted in some way, whether to alcohol or other substances, to other people or to certain activities may be doing so to cope with feelings of inferiority or rejection by society, and of course these addictions only make matters worse. I'm speaking here of one of the worst results but I'm sure many of us can identify with either a clear feeling of not being very worthy, or with times when we've felt that others' actions are telling us we don't matter very much. Low self-esteem can also be the cause of depression and some psychiatric illnesses.

For my part, one of the things I've had to work on was feeling that I don't matter and dealing with the way that's made me react in certain circumstances. It probably stems from childhood when I wasn't allowed to express any negative feelings, and it rears its ugly head when I don't hear from a friend as often as I'd like or I get left out of conversations or decision-making.

Something I come across a lot with many is the need to please others in order to be loved and this can lead to people exhausting themselves in service to others to the detriment of their own health and well-being. It stems from not feeling good enough (very low self-esteem). Rejection or betrayal are things we almost all have to endure at some stage in life to some degree or another, and the state of our self-esteem will determine how well we can cope with it and how we emerge on the other side of it. These are frequently the cause of self-esteem problems in the first place, especially when they happen at a very early, formative age. Time and circumstances can help to heal any dents in one's image of oneself, but working on liking oneself and giving up judgements are exercises that can do a lot of good too. I've found some exercises really helpful for myself and others, and have progressed now to knowing that I really *do* matter, whatever anyone else thinks and, if others don't acknowledge this, it *almost* always doesn't bother me. I admit that age does play some part in this as I certainly worry a lot less these days about what others think of me than I did in younger days, but I am sure that the work has paid off too.

## NOTICING OUR REACTIONS

This is something that becomes possible when we are practising awareness—listening to our thoughts and noticing how our body is feeling. Strong experiences and conditioning that have impacted us from early childhood and through life may be triggered unexpectedly in current circumstances or by certain people. Our reactions may be far from positive or helpful to ourselves, but, by being aware, we will notice this and can use them to explore how they might be affecting our self-esteem, and possibly reinforcing unhelpful ideas we have about our place in the world. If it's found that they stem from serious traumas of the past, then some professional help might be advisable.

## THE CLUES

Let's look at some of the give-away clues that can indicate poor self-esteem:

- **Feeling you don't matter, and mistakenly proving this to yourself through another's actions.**
- **Always putting others' needs before your own in order to appear good.**
- **Lacking the confidence to try new things or worrying unduly about doing so.**
- **Often tending to feel you're a victim in some way or other.**
- **Criticising others to make you feel better.**
- **Believing you don't deserve to be happy, prosperous, healthy, loved, etc.**
- **Thinking everyone is better than you are in some way.**
- **Beating yourself up or feeling guilty over mistakes, carelessness, etc.**
- **Being indecisive through fear of failure, disappointment, or regret.**
- **Trying to change yourself in order to please others and/or be loved.**
- **Calling yourself names or making derogatory comments about yourself.**
- **Incorrectly taking other people's actions and comments personally.**
- **Avoiding friendships or relationships lest the others discover your failings.**
- **Boasting or bragging to make yourself appear superior to others.**

**Exercise 1:**

**I'd like you now to think carefully about each of the above habits and see if they apply to you, making a list of those that do. Keep the list for using later in this section. Once you get thinking, you might come up with some other habits and feelings of your own that you realise are to do with self-esteem and these can be added to your list.**

So far this may have been sounding a bit depressing and daunting, but, of course, our programming hasn't all been bad news. You may have been fortunate enough to have had a very positive childhood with lots of praise and encouragement. You might have been guided in your education to focus on your talents or been given positive feedback on your accomplishments. On the other hand, you may have already worked on and seen the value of positive thinking about yourself and discovered how much more comfortable you now feel about being you. The degree to which this has all happened will have determined your current level of self-esteem.

An important fact to remember is that self-esteem must come from within in order to be solid and unmovable. Building it on status, material wealth, fame or the opinions of others is like building on sand because any of these could change or disappear completely. We need to feel worthy simply because we are here, and we are our unique self. We are an essential part of life's jigsaw and as necessary and entitled to be here as everyone else. We might spend the whole of life being miserable because we're waiting for others' approval, or even to be noticed, while we could be getting on with living life to the full in a way that brings us joy, which, in my belief, is what we're here to do.

It's another case of having to rewire connections in the brain concerning self-esteem and, as I said, these have been many years in the making. We have been making neural pathways all our lives and we create them when we learn anything, whether consciously or subconsciously. They are the body's way of maintaining habitual behaviour and will by now be thick and strong. Disconnecting these is not easy and it takes dedicated effort to create new ones that serve us better. Please don't be discouraged by the amount of practice required as the result will be very well worth it.

## ACCENTUATE THE POSITIVE

Before we start the process of discovering your negative self-talk and where any self-esteem problems have come from, I want to help you focus on what you like about yourself. If liking yourself sounds a big ask at this stage, at least decide to find some aspects of yourself that you wouldn't want to change, whether these were formed by childhood or later conditioning, or consciously developed by yourself.

**Exercise 2:**

**Take your time to find and list at least five things that you like about yourself or that you do or have done well. If you can get a good friend or family member to help, the list will almost certainly grow longer. In fact, it's a lovely exercise to do for each other as we can be very poor at recognising our good features and talents. Here are some examples that I hope will help to get you started:**

- **good listener**
- **good cook**
- **cheerful company**
- **hard working**
- **eat a healthy diet**
- **stylish dresser**
- **good organiser**
- **talented artist**
- **good parent**
- **helpful/loyal friend**
- **clever/popular at school.**

**Having created your list, which might grow over time as you notice or remember more items to add (keep it safe, please), you are now going to strengthen these beliefs in a way that might remind you of detention from school days when the method was used as**

**a means of correcting unhelpful behaviour. This will introduce you to the use of affirmations as another helpful tool.**

* * *

**Exercise 3:**

**Write out each item on the list at least three times (more times for any that were given by your helper, and you're not totally convinced about) in a short sentence such as:**

- **I am a generous friend/I am generous with my time.**
- **I always cook delicious and healthy meals.**
- **I was at school (and still am) a hard-working student.**
- **People love to hear me sing.**

**Concentrate fully on each sentence as you write it.**

Something I've been using for a long time now, and continue to use, is my little book of '**Strokes and Hugs**'. It's a small, pretty notebook in which I write the occasional genuine compliment or praise that I receive from someone, and I keep it in my bedside drawer to read through at any time that I feel the need of a boost to my self-esteem. The entries range from compliments about my appearance or my home, such as "Your hair is such a beautiful colour", to comments such as "You have been such a true inspiration to me". We are so conditioned not to be vain or proud that we can find it hard to receive compliments and praise, but that's not being very being very kind to ourselves. We spend a lot of time and effort in trying to be the best we can be, so why not remind ourselves now and then of how well we are doing and reward ourselves for our continued effort? If you like the idea, why not start a little strokes and hugs book of your own? It will encourage you to accept the good words you receive as well as giving you further boosts, both as you write them out and again when you read them now and then.

Now, because we are going on to look at negative input we've received from others during our lives, I'd like you first to give credit, if you can, to the origins of these positive traits and talents that you have now acknowledged. It can sometimes be all too easy to blame others for our shortcomings and misfortunes but there will almost certainly have been some positive effects from our experiences. We are not doing the following exercise 4 in order to negate all your own abilities and efforts to develop your positive characteristics, but to show how positive statements and encouragement can affect how we think and feel about ourselves.

**Exercise 4:**

**Consider each item on your list and see if you can find its origin. For example:**

- **Is your accomplished piano playing partly due to your parents paying for you to have lessons as a child?**
- **Did a teacher notice your interest in mechanical things and encourage you to develop the talent you now have in that field?**
- **Has a friend who is good at listening become a role model for you to develop the same trait?**
- **Were you sometimes pushed out of your comfort zone only to discover that you could achieve what you had thought impossible, thus gaining the courage to give things a try, however daunting?**
- **Were you praised for being pretty/clever/creative/a good friend/appreciative, etc.?**

I should take a little break now, before moving on. Reinforcing the positive work we've done will be worthwhile, before exploring the origins of our negative feelings about ourselves.

## DISCOVERING THE NEGATIVES

**A little warning**:We have moved in this section into some challenging territory and the following exercises should not be entered into lightly. Please read them through to see what's required before you tackle them, and allow yourself plenty of time when you are feeling robust enough to deal with any deep and difficult emotions that come up. Consider whether you prefer to do this alone or with an understanding and supportive friend, relative or even a professional counsellor. It will help you to keep all the lists you make, not only to add to as and when you think of more things but also to use for reprogramming purposes.

**Exercise 5:**

**I now want you to find the origins of any limiting or discouraging beliefs you have about yourself. We do this by looking back through our lives at what people said about us, or how they behaved towards us, especially the people who matter most to us. To help you get started, find the clues you wrote out near the beginning of this section. Here too are a few examples of the kind of comments you might have received as a child, or even since then.**

- **You're just a lazy...**
- **You'll never be able to...**
- **Why can't you be like your sister/brother?**

- **We're not interested in what you think.**
- **You were a mistake.**
- **You're stupid.**
- **Why can't you be more...?**
- **You can't sing/dance/teach...**
- **Why do you always look such a mess?**
- **What did I do wrong to deserve you?**
- **You'll always be a loser.**

**Make a list of any that you recognise and any others you can think of, and think carefully about how these statements have affected or still do affect your behaviour now. It's not the easiest of exercises but, with the motivation to reprogram the beliefs that are not helping you, I'm sure you will manage to list some things. If you have a 'growth buddy' who knows you well, they may help you to see the areas that need work.**

By the way, not every negative comment will have had a bad effect. I was told I'd never have the patience to teach but I am quite a patient person and have spent a lot of my working life teaching in some form or other. At this stage, you need to find the ones that still affect you adversely now.

**As this could be a fairly challenging section to work on, it might be a good idea now to split the exercises by having a break here. It will also give you time to think about and**

work on the lists you've already made, possibly adding more to them. By now I hope that you can see how any negative conditioning you've received is affecting how you feel about yourself and will begin to notice how this affects your emotions and your actions in everyday life. In the meantime, you might like to read a little idea of mine over the page that I feel is appropriate at this stage.

# THE UNIVERSAL JIGSAW

Do you ever wonder why you're here or whether you matter? Or maybe you feel less significant than others who seem to do great works or take big roles in the play of life. Do you worry that you might be missing the point, or feel like an 'also ran' without any great purpose? We all too often judge ourselves as better or worse than others for some reason while we really have no justification for our views. When I find myself tempted to do this, I like to think of life as a jigsaw, and that the universe needs every one of us for it to be a complete creation, just as a jigsaw needs every single piece of itself.

Each jigsaw piece has its own shape and function and each one is essential to make up the picture. Some pieces have a lot of indents. They need those others with the 'sticky-out' bits to fit nicely into those gaps, just as some people's gifts and talents are needed by others. Some pieces have no holes but only outward pointing shapes to fill others' gaps, in the same way that people vary between the totally self-sufficient, helpful, and outgoing to those who are sick, needy or vulnerable. They need each other to complete the picture.

Then there are the edges. These all have a difference about them from the majority, and can show up rather distinctly in the jumble of pieces. We all know of some folk who stand out in the crowd.

Sometimes in a jigsaw there are large areas of plain colour. It might be a plain grey sky and it's very difficult to put together the pieces here as they all look so similar. There may be a lot that are identical in shape and all the same clear colour. Individually they may look dull and uninteresting. However, if one of these pieces is missing on completion of the picture, it shows up horribly and spoils the whole effect.

Then there are pieces with bright colours, distinct markings or important features such as part of a flower, a bird's beak or a person's hand, and it's easy to see where these fit compared with those that are vague and enigmatic. Whichever type is missing, it spoils the end results and causes the picture to be incomplete.

When it comes to those who are trying to reconstruct the picture, they don't all have the same methods and preferences. Some 'puzzlers' go for the edges first while others prefer to start with all the obvious, easier areas. Then there are those who much prefer the challenge of the vague bits. The analogy here is that all the bits are equally likeable in their own way.

The jigsaw was originally created as a whole picture before being sawn into its separate parts. The aim of the exercise is for each piece to find its correct place, connect to its neighbours comfortably and fulfil its part of the scene so that the puzzle becomes once more an integrated whole. Each piece has its unique, specific place and every piece matters equally—just as we each have our part to play, whether we think we are dull, or interesting, or whatever adjective we give ourselves.

# SELF-ESTEEM (PART 2)

So, getting back to our work on self-esteem, another route of investigation we can use to find what is damaging ours is to look at how we put ourselves down when we admire or criticise others. Yes, these two opposites can be clues to how we value ourselves. The next exercise needs time and some honest delving within yourself but can be very illuminating.

When we make negative judgements about others (aloud or in our heads) we are usually doing so in an effort to make ourselves feel better, although we are not consciously aware of this, of course. For example, "He's so lazy"; "She's too fat", "They are so messy". The fact that we are judging already makes us feel superior or better than another and enables our ego to feel righteous (in these cases industrious, slim and tidy). You may say that it does also remind us of our preferences and how we don't want to be, but does it always? It could be that you struggle to stay slim because you think others will like you better that way. You may not allow yourself to be 'lazy' because of your programming, whereas you would dearly love to give yourself a day off sometimes (and why not?), or you would love to be a bit less tidy all the time. All of this is going on subconsciously inside your mind because your low self-esteem prevents you feeling good enough just as you are.

So now we need to do some more thinking to discover how we really think of ourselves.

**Exercise 6:**

a. **Think about and list what you most often criticise in others—both individuals you know and general groups. For example: laziness, bossiness, timidity, extravagance...**
b. **Go back to each one and honestly ask yourself if you ever criticise yourself for any of them. Do you feel you are lazy, too forceful, less confident than others, etc.? Put a mark by any you have to admit to. We'll come back to deal with the list later.**

Oddly enough, another way to spot our self-esteem issues is to notice what we admire in others. It may seem strange that admiring others can be harmful to our own self-worth, but this can be the case if it leads us to make critical comparisons between them and us. For example, "She's much prettier than I am", "I wish I were as funny as he is", "My singing is hopeless compared to her beautiful voice". I'm not saying we shouldn't admire others—it's admirable—but it's worth looking at where it stems from and whether it amounts to a criticism of ourselves, especially if there's envy in there somewhere.

**Exercise 7:**

a. **In the same way as you did for exercise 6, find and list what you admire in people generally and in any particular people you know, or know of (such as celebrities).**
b. **Put marks by the items that have an element of envy in them or in cases where you feel yourself inferior.**

You might discover from these exercises that you do actually have a low opinion of yourself or feel inadequate in some areas. This is constantly damaging your self-esteem, which may be preventing you from fulfilling all your potential. Your awareness will enable you to determine whether this is the case. As I said earlier, the degree to which we accept or like ourselves affects our interactions with life and other people, and certainly affects our inner calm. The way out of it is through awareness again and watching our thoughts as they try to run away out of control. We need to catch ourselves criticising or admiring others and doing these inner comparisons, and make a point of looking into why we have these opinions of ourselves. When we spot these damaging thoughts about ourselves, we can counteract them with positive reminders of what we are good at and our valuable characteristics.

## MAKING NEW PATHWAYS

This is where you are going back to make use of all those lists.

**Exercise 8:**

a. **First of all, turn to the list of the negative or discouraging comments you received from others ('Self-esteem Part 1', exercise 5). Alongside each of the statements that you think still affects you now, write positive sentences that you feel would have been more helpful. Try to really rephrase the original, such as "You'll never be able to..." changes to "You can achieve anything you set your mind to" or "Give it a go". Try to imagine how different it would feel to be given this encouragement.**
b. **Now write each one of these positive statements out again but in the first person. E.g. "I can achieve anything I set my mind to","At least I can give it a go".**

**I find that this exercise has a deeper effect if I get myself into the 'checking-in' state—calm, relaxed, breathing slowly and deeply, and in touch with my real self. If you get into this state, you should be able to feel how uplifting it is to hear positive statements or encouraging words about yourself.**

## AFFIRMATIONS

What you have written out for yourself in the above exercise is some affirmations. These can work really well for some people, and do so for me. Thanks to Louise Hay's book, *You Can Heal Your Life,* using affirmations was one of the first tools I ever used, and I still do. They have been in general use for years now in the fields of self-improvement, life-coaching, and some therapies. We don't have to believe them, but they must be positive statements and repeated often. Apparently, it is a fact that our subconscious will believe whatever we tell it with emotion or conviction. The method I use is to write out some positive statements that counteract any problem I am having, such as lack of confidence or feeling I don't matter. I choose the ones that resonate best with me and write them on a card, which I put where I will see it often throughout the day. Whenever I come across it, I repeat the affirmations—out loud, if possible—a few times, while getting in touch with the feeling it creates.

I believe that the least effect an affirmation can have is to keep in mind a goal that I have, and bring my mind back from racing off somewhere into unhelpful thoughts. For example, "Day by day I am becoming more aware and peaceful". Before you go on to make affirmations related to your other lists, I'd like to offer you some general ones that people usually find helpful. By the end of this whole section, you may have made a lot more, but I recommend that for a week or so you concentrate on no more than three of the following. These should have a boosting effect on how you feel about yourself and put you in a better frame of mind to tackle the more specific and personal ones.

**Exercise 9:**

**Write out the following affirmations and read each one out loud:**

- **I am good enough just as I am.**
- **Others' opinions of me can't hurt me.**
- **I am a confident and capable person.**
- **I am a vital part of the web of life.**
- **I am a good... (parent, employee, son, daughter, speaker, friend, etc.).**
- **I can handle whatever life brings me.**

**Choose two or three and write them on a small card that you can place where you will see it frequently. As often as possible, say your chosen affirmations out loud, really thinking about what they mean.**

* * *

**Exercise 10:**

a. **Go back to your lists from exercises 6 and 7 in this section and make up appropriate affirmations to counteract the negative beliefs you discovered you have about yourself.**

**b. Again, choose just a few to work on until you begin to notice an improvement in how you feel about this aspect of yourself.**

In a way, affirmations are about talking to ourselves in a positive way, which reminds me of another way we do our self-esteem no good at all—critical self-talk. I know we've already looked into how we compare ourselves to others in a critical way, but how many times do we call ourselves names like "you silly fool", "what an idiot", etc.? Whereas we've had no say in what others have called us over the years, we are totally in control of what we say to ourselves. There's not a lot of point in working to override those early detrimental comments if we're going to continue putting ourselves down by calling ourselves names on a daily basis. So, please, from now on, watch out for the language you use to yourself about yourself, and try to be kinder. If you do forget something or make a mistake, and want to make a mental comment, phrase it in gentle words as you would for a small child, e.g. "Whoops! You didn't mean to do that, did you?" or "A little memory blip there, I think". Be your own best friend.

## AND NOW FOR A TIMELY REMINDER

I'm hoping that, by now, you are feeling and appreciating the connection between what you think and how your body feels, and agreeing that your body is your buddy. Well, even when it comes to the sometimes serious and challenging work of improving self-esteem, the body can be brought in to help. Just as the subconscious believes whatever we say to ourselves, whether it's true or not, we can also influence what we believe about ourselves through our bodies. It involves using the tool I call 'act as if...' (as described in the step, Our Body is Our Buddy) and simply requires that we move, hold ourselves and walk about as if we feel confident and self-assured. When we do this often enough, consciously, it becomes a habit, and we begin to become aware of the feeling that goes with it. Maybe you can picture someone you know or have seen who walks with a confident gait. This probably involves them holding their head high, with shoulders relaxed and back. They will lead forward with their chest open rather than compressed and they will have a loose, relaxed walk, swinging their arms easily as they go. Remember too that a smiling face is always more confident than a frowning or scowling one.

In order to appreciate how this works, try the following exercise:

**Exercise 11:**

**Where you are sitting now, straighten your back so that your chest expands. Relax your breathing. Hold your head straight, lengthening your neck as if a string is pulling your head up from above. Lower your shoulders, look around you slowly and smile. Notice whether you feel any different inside.**

Hopefully, this gives you a little taster of what it feels like to be confident if that's not your usual way of feeling. A favourite game of mine, when I have the time to watch people moving about or when out walking, is to notice a person's walk and to imagine how that person is feeling by imagining myself walking the same way. It's better still if I can actually copy the walk without being noticed. If you try this some time, you will notice how good it is to see a confident, relaxed walk and how you might feel some compassion for someone looking timid, depressed, or self-conscious. These latter folk will be recognisable by being slightly round-shouldered (contracting their chest), arms hanging fairly still as they walk or they may be taking small, uncertain steps for no obvious reason. A lack of spring in the step can be another sign of low self-esteem, and some people almost lean back as they walk as if they are afraid of what's coming next. The variations are endless.

Here's another little exercise to help you to get the feeling of how this works before you start making the necessary physical changes that I hope you're going to try for yourself.

**Exercise 12:**

**Get yourself into a relaxed and quiet frame of mind by doing a 'checking-in' or taking a few deep breaths and imagine that your name has been called at a big event as the winner of a prestigious award. You have to walk up to the stage to collect it while your friends, family and the rest of the audience applaud you. Stay with the visualisation and notice how you feel and how you hold your body as you walk forward.**

**If these exercises are working for you, why not stand up now to try out a confident pose and go on to take a few steps, at least. If you have somewhere to have a good walk around, so much the better, and then it would be good to remind yourself, whenever you can, to walk and hold yourself in this confident manner. Don't forget the smile because I believe it makes any exercise more effective by releasing those valuable endorphins. If there's a mirror nearby, it's great to smile at yourself as if at another person.**

As a final note I must just say that, apart from simply making us feel better about ourselves, improving our self-esteem has many other benefits. It means we'll take better care of ourselves physically as well as emotionally. This in turn will enable us to make more of a contribution to life and to get more out of it by becoming more of who we really are. When we think poorly of ourselves, we tend to criticise and judge others as a way of making us feel better. Consequently we are unable to truly love others until we learn to love ourselves. Another great benefit is that we're more inclined to allow ourselves to do and have the things we really love when we convince ourselves that we are really worthy of them. There is also the danger that our low self-esteem might lead us to search for a special other to 'complete' us with the traits we lack, or to boost our feelings about ourselves by their admiration. Neither of these is a good reason for entering a relationship. I hope you'll agree that all these reasons make the effort required in this section well worthwhile.

## REMINDERS

1. Keep noticing when you criticise or admire someone to check whether you are (a) really criticising yourself or (b) compensating for something you feel you lack.
2. Watch out for critical self-talk and rephrase whenever you notice it.
3. Create a positive and confident walk that makes you feel good about yourself and practise it whenever you can.
4. Re-read your list of good points and keep adding to it as you notice more of your strengths.
5. Make up and repeat often some affirmations to help with the aspects of self-esteem you most want to work on.
6. Smile at yourself every time you catch sight of an image of yourself somewhere.

# SELF-ESTEEM AFTERTHOUGHT

I am aware that, during or following our work on self-esteem, there will be readers who struggle with the concept of feeling proud or confident, and even more of loving ourselves. We therefore need to look at self-pride vs arrogance and self-love vs narcissism. It is possible, and desirable, to love yourself while maintaining (or cultivating) humility.

There is a definite difference between being humble or modest and being self-effacing. The latter may be a sign of low self-esteem whereas being humble acknowledges that we have our own place in the world and the right to be here without placing ourselves above others.

It's sometimes easier to understand something by contrasting it with its opposite. We live in a world of paradox, after all, where we recognise light thanks to darkness and shadow, and we are surrounded by the yin and yang, feminine and masculine of everything. The opposite of humility is arrogance. Arrogance has people wanting to have the last word because they believe they are right. In fact, they can't bear to be wrong. Should it be proven that they are wrong—have quoted the wrong facts or mis-remembered something—they can barely admit it to themselves, let alone to anyone else. The arrogant don't like to be told anything they already know (or think they do) and, when that happens, they have to make it clear that they already knew it. If it is new to them, they will rarely admit that to be so. They like to preach to others and show off their knowledge in rigid dogmatic fashion and often enjoy an argument or discussion in the hope and belief that they can win.

The humble, on the other hand, may know a great deal and be very wise but just get on with using what they know to go about their own lives. They are happy to help or advise if asked, but in a gentle, encouraging way. Humble folk give opinions if required without insisting that their views are right. They are usually open-minded and prepared to listen to others' points of view. When the humble receive a compliment, they accept it with grace and gratitude or total surprise, which demonstrates more self-love than the denying or minimising comments that the self-effacing personalities would make.

**Exercise:**

**Can you imagine anyone you know who fits either of these descriptions? Can you feel how it is to be with either of them? Can you tell which description better fits yourself?**

Humility/modesty doesn't mean that you can't be proud of your achievements and recognise your gifts and talents, but you don't need to brag about them. It includes a degree of gratitude somehow for these and an awareness that we are all blessed with different degrees of intelligence and knowledge according to our circumstances and genes. Having learned a bit more or having a better memory or quicker wit doesn't make someone a better person or give him or her any valid reason to feel superior to others.

Humility recognises truth and authenticity. We feel humbled when we see an example of great human spirit or courage, I suppose, because it shows what we are all capable of but most of us don't achieve. Our modesty acknowledges that whatever we are or achieve is a result of being human rather than just being this individual, so we take no personal credit for it. Although they may not be consciously aware of it, I believe that humble folk are operating more from their real selves/higher selves/souls, while the arrogant are very much in their egos and operating without awareness. Of course we need egos to operate in life, but living only from that state is when our thoughts and emotions take us over and old conditioning is triggered, such as the need to inflate ourselves to protect our low self-esteem.

# THINGS ALONG THE WAY—1

**There are some topics that have been instrumental in me finding more tranquillity, but that I don't consider *essential*, but helpful in achieving inner peace. I hope that, by giving just a taster of how these subjects have helped me or others, you might be encouraged to either give them a try, or to look into them in more detail to see if they appeal to you in any way.**

## MEDITATION

I feel that I must begin with meditation as it was where I started many years ago when it felt as if my life was falling apart. Because I was falling apart inside, I looked around for helping strategies and began by enrolling for a meditation course at the local evening class centre. Apart from teaching me many ways to meditate, the course opened me up to a wide world of alternative therapies, practices and beliefs that were all new to me.

I have used different forms of meditation ever since but not as a routine, and this is how this handbook came about. Because I don't seem to be cut out for sitting for 20 minutes or longer twice a day, every day (and have come across many others who feel the same), I explored the possibility of creating the same peaceful and even blissful states on a more permanent basis. This is what I have been passing on here. The very idea of finding the two 20-minute periods a day that are recommended often meets with resistance from the majority of people who feel far too busy keeping up with the rush of today's busy world. This doesn't mean it wouldn't do them the world of good, of course. They could find themselves losing that sense of urgency but, sadly, a lot are unlikely to stay with the discipline.

However, by doing the exercises I've been offering here, you have touched on many of the types of meditation without making them the only tool for achieving your calm peacefulness. Any of these can be expanded into a longer sitting practice:

- following the breath
- body scan
- visualization
- reciting affirmations
- relaxation
- being with a pain or emotion
- focusing on a 'smiley'.

I started trying to meditate with the mistaken belief that the aim was to empty my mind. I believe many others share this idea, which can lead them to the conclusion that they are hopeless at it and cause them to give up the practice. The actual aim of a meditation session is to avoid getting *involved* in our thoughts, and, instead, watching them float across the mind like clouds in the sky or leaves on a stream. You will notice that this is different from what we've been aiming to achieve here, as I feel that there are times when it is worth looking at the thoughts that create emotions in us, finding ways to deal with the unhelpful ones. The truth of the matter is that there is call for both methods.

Here is an exercise to turn breathing awareness into a meditation session in order for you to see whether you'd like to look further into the practice. (You will have to memorise it or record it before you start.) If you do think meditation is for you, it shouldn't be difficult to find a book, course, workshop or website to help you expand the practice.

**Exercise:**

1. **Set aside at least ten minutes when you won't be disturbed, away from other people, television, telephones, etc. Twenty or more minutes make a better period, but you may want to work up to this.**
2. **Lie flat or sit upright with your spine straight and nothing crossed (hands at your sides, if lying, or in your lap, if sitting).**
3. **Close your eyes.**
4. **Start to watch your breath going in and out of the body. Some like to count each breath while others silently recite "Breathing in; breathing out" or "Relaxation in; tension out".**

5. **As thoughts float into your mind, visualise them floating out again, without getting caught up in them. If it helps, you could categorise them into past, future, etc. before letting them go. Return to the breath.**
6. **As you become aware of sensations in your body such as an itch or discomfort, just observe it and return to your breath. (If it becomes too distracting, do something about it and then return to your breath.)**
7. **Continue this for whatever time you have set and then gradually bring yourself to an awareness of your surroundings and open your eyes.**

Some people prefer to have a visualisation for their meditation time, giving them a focus beyond the breath. If you choose to try this, always start by totally relaxing the body and taking some deep breaths to get into the '**real me**' state, then conjure up your own vision such as watching a stream go by, lying on a beach in the warm sun or flying over a beautiful landscape. (There are millions of options.) Alternatively, find a recorded spoken visualisation to follow.

# FIRST AID FOR EMOTIONS

I hope that you are now getting into the habit of watching all the variety of thoughts that assail you during the course of the day, and noticing when they are distracting you from the present moment or leading you into a negative emotion or even stress. Although we've been looking at ways to keep an eye on them, that doesn't mean that we instantly have the means to control them all and, likewise, the emotions they cause. It may be that you are taking charge of your thoughts so that a lot of the emotions that used to cause you stress and unhappiness are not getting a chance to surface so much now, but it takes time to create new habits and forge new pathways in the brain. So, in the meantime, it can be helpful to have strategies for dealing with some of the more troubling emotions. When we find ourselves suffering or struggling within, we already have some techniques that we can use:

1. Stop and take some deep breaths.
2. Scan the body to see where the physical tension is and release it.
3. Notice the thought that triggered the uncomfortable feeling and see if you can change it to a more positive one or implement the appropriate 'cure'.
4. Name the emotion, e.g. "This is fear. This is anger."

5. Stay with the emotion if you can, fully feeling it but not acting on it (unless, of course, there is a real physical danger from which you need to escape!), and not feeding it with more of the same negative thoughts.

Quite often, simply carrying out these steps will be enough to bring calm and clear the mind, freeing us from whatever the bad feeling was. Furthermore, each time we practise this routine, it will get easier and eventually become a habitual way of dealing with the internal negativity. However, I have found a few more handy tools to help with general and specific emotions that you might like to consider adding to your tool kit. You will probably find that some may suit you more than others.

One general rescuer (which can also help those with poor self-esteem) is not to label yourself with the negative emotion. Rather than saying “I’m angry”, say to yourself something like “I sense anger in me” or “Anger is here” or “Anger is passing through”. The latter one is especially helpful as it reminds you that nothing is permanent and the anger, fear, jealousy, etc. will pass. Remember, we are not our emotions. Having acknowledged how you’re feeling, you could proceed with the five steps above, which should at least reduce your suffering somewhat.

A way of dealing with emotions that I find particularly useful is writing. No, I’m not recommending that you have pen and paper always at the ready, or disappear in the midst of a discussion or tricky situation to write about your difficult feelings, but it can be an excellent way of releasing emotions in a safe and controlled manner when circumstances allow. It’s a way of voicing what you are feeling without actually voicing it out loud and without the risk of some other party feeling hurt. Writing a letter to someone you are angry with or having some other difficulty about, and then destroying the letter without them seeing it, can be quite therapeutic. Even a passive emotion, such as sadness or loneliness, can be helped by writing out a sort of conversation with yourself. It works better than having that conversation just in the head, because we have to slow down our thoughts in order to write them. It can be surprising to discover what is the root cause of the bad feeling.

Of course, if you have a growth buddy or close, trustworthy friend, who will listen to you without judgement, it is hard to beat talking about any emotional difficulties you are having. Be careful, though, to do this in a constructive way, seeking to find out how you are making yourself suffer through unhelpful thinking or reacting in an old, conditioned way. I find that speaking out a problem helps me to see the cause of it more clearly for myself, often not even requiring input from the other person. Remember, this is not like asking advice, but asking them to support you while you clarify what you are going through.

Your next steps will be specific to the emotion involved and the circumstance, but let's look at a few options here that can be adapted to a range of scenarios. These are certainly not the only ways of dealing with situations, but simply some that I and others have found helpful. An important starting point is to remind yourself that it's not the event that caused the emotion, but your perception and thought about it.

**Attacked by someone's angry words.** Try getting in touch with your calm centre so that you can respond rather than react automatically. The long-standing advice to count to ten is still relevant, as long as you accompany your counting with some deep breaths.

If you can go a step further, you could internally send the person love and compassion for the bad way they must be feeling.

**Anger with a friend or family member.** Try to see why their action caused you to react that way. Which 'buttons' in you did they press, and where did that originate in your past? If possible, replace the angry thought with gratitude for having him/her in your life. If you go deeply enough inside, you may find your love for them is stronger than the anger you were feeling.

**Anger for a cause or over a situation. C**heck first whether it's really your business or someone else's. Are you fighting reality, in which case you can accept, leave or make a change/take action (once you are thinking clearly again and operating from your calm centre). In the latter case, anger has been used constructively to give energy to an action.

**Fear of failure.** Believe that you could be as capable as those who have achieved the same feat (speaking in public, running a marathon, cooking a meal for a group of friends, etc.). Use positive affirmations and visualise yourself completing the task and how good you will feel then. It's also worth reminding yourself that you will do your best, and life is not a competition.

**Impatience.** Remember that life is all about change. Whatever is delaying the result you're impatient for, it will pass. Notice how your impatience is affecting your body, as it is sure to make you tense, and resolve to be kinder to yourself by slowing down.

**Frustration.** This arises when we feel out of control and is a mixture of impatience and anger. It can be dealt with by using some of the solutions for these two and can be helped particularly by some physical exercise and deep breathing.

**Resentment.** This is like festering after an injury and is a particularly harmful emotion because of the effects it can have on us. It amounts to us feeling a victim, causes us to dwell on negative thoughts and sometimes includes a desire for vengeance. Because it amounts to something 'eating away at us', it can obviously be very harmful to the body, even though we may not be aware of any physical problems at the time. Try to notice how the feeling is preventing you from enjoying the present moment by keeping you in negativity, and resolve to let it go. It means you are fighting reality or dwelling in the past, so use the cures for these. The physical letting-go exercise that you have learnt can also help. (Swinging both arms, raising one and dropping it suddenly with a sharp out-breath.)

**Depression.** This can, of course, be a clinical condition that needs medical and/or psychological help, but we can find ourselves temporarily depressed over a current situation or even have a black cloud over us that needs to be investigated for its cause. The effect of depression is usually lethargy and finding no joy in whatever we are doing. Whatever you discover about the origin of the feeling, there are a few things that can lift you out of this negativity. You could get on with something practical that can be easily accomplished and praise yourself for its completion. You could try 'acting as if' you feel more positive about things until you do. Of particular use is a list of everything good in your life for which you feel grateful. If the depression is not too deep, thinking about your 'smileys' should brighten your mood. Physical exercise—even a short, brisk walk—will release endorphins to help you feel more positive.

**Jealousy.** This comes from insecurity and fear. We feel that we need a certain someone to love us or even just to be in our life and we go into a degree of panic if we perceive this state is being threatened. We might be afraid of not being 'number 1' to them or having to share their love with another. Some ways to avoid this feeling might be:

- to work on improving your own self-esteem so that you don't *need* someone's love, attention, or approval in order to feel good about yourself
- to accept you can't change reality or another person's behaviour or preferences
- not to let your mind make up worrying stories about what is going on.

**Envy.** If I'm wanting something that another has—be it material possession or personal talent or feature, or even success, I'm fighting reality again and making myself unhappy. I have seen envy within groups result in the person envied being unpleasantly or even cruelly treated by others, and those on both sides of this sometimes fail to see that the root cause of this behaviour is envy.

One obvious cure for this is to have gratitude for all that we do have. It could also be put to good use by turning the object of envy into a goal to pursue in a positive frame of mind.

Of course, there are many more emotions we can suffer from with just as many other ways of dealing with them. I realise that I have only scratched the surface here, but I'm hoping that the skills you've picked up so far will help you to work out your own correction methods when urgent help is needed. Otherwise, remember that it's always better to stay with an emotion until it diminishes or, even better, not to let our minds lead into the negativity in the first place.

I hope you are becoming convinced by now, through becoming aware of how the mind works, that creating a calm and happy feeling is a choice we can make and a habit we can develop. It does seem to me that the human race's ability to think has been both a huge blessing for our evolution but also a dangerous tool on both a personal and global scale. The rest of the animal kingdom still operates mostly from instinct and, because of the way their brains have evolved, most animals have only small areas devoted to emotions. So far as we know, we seem to be the only species that has the ability to cause our own inner suffering through what we think but now, thankfully, we have also realised that, with awareness, we can avoid doing this.

It would great if you could share my vision of this awareness practice spreading from person to person. It's easy to see how negative energy can pass on from one to another. For example, someone dwelling on the feeling that they've been wronged somehow snaps at another who then gets in a bad mood and, on arriving home, finds fault with their partner or children, and so it goes on. If the first one in the chain had dealt skilfully with their feeling rather than just reacting automatically or letting hurt or vengeful thoughts take over, there would have been no ripples of negativity to spread to others. When more of us become able to stay calm and live from our wise real selves, the more chance there will be of peace prevailing. Peace begins with the individual—with each one of us.

# AWARENESS REMINDER

We've been working on being aware for some while now and I hope you are noticing the difference it makes to so many aspects of everyday life. It occurred to me recently to list all those aspects I could think of where awareness is helping me. In some ways the list can be endless, but, as each item occurred to me, I stopped to consider what I learned and how I benefit from the awareness of it.

**Exercise:**

**Before you look at my list, I suggest you start a list of your own and here is an example of how the exercise worked for me.**

**What am I aware of?**
*My judgements of others.*

**How does this awareness help me?**
*It helps me to break the habit. I now notice that I'm judging; remind myself that it's none of my business how they are; remember they have*

*had and are having a different experience of life; look for any mirrors of my own behaviour (such as aspects of myself that I don't like) ; send them love; forgive myself for the mistake.*

**Now start to make your own list of where awareness can help you. I recommend that you don't rush through this exercise because it acts as an excellent revision of all that we are trying to achieve with these practices. You could even jot down items as they occur to you, going back to them later to consider how becoming more aware is helping you.**

**Once you've had a go at this, you might like to see some more of my list.**

**I am now, or am at least trying to, stay aware of:**

- **my thoughts**
- **when I've gone off balance**
- **my feelings**
- **how I find some personalities difficult**
- **my surroundings**
- **my intentions**
- **other people's needs**
- **my talents and gifts**
- **what brings me most joy**
- **the present moment**

- **my still, calm centre**
- **my truth**
- **my resistances**
- **my attachments and expectations**
- **my blessings**
- **my unhelpful habits and beliefs**
- **how my body's feeling**
- **when I need to rest or be alone.**

**If you notice areas here that you can't yet add to your own list, these might be worth you working on next.**

## EXTENDING AWARENESS

It seems that, the longer I take to pass on what I've learned, the more appears for me to find out. My latest discovery, which has recently been researched and proven scientifically, is that we have a part of our brain relating to both spirituality and depression, and that, the more of a sense we have of being part of something greater than just our individual self, the less susceptible we become to feelings of depression.

This spirituality does not require a following of any religion or dogma, or even a belief in any 'higher' being. At its simplest it can be a sense of there being something more than the physical self and material world of things around us. This feeling can be triggered when we wonder at nature or are captivated by music or any form of art. We might have a feeling of belonging, being part of something greater, a connection with others or even a oneness with all living beings through our shared experience of life.

It is a good starting point to consider that we are all made up of mind, body, and spirit, and then to notice when something moves us, brings us joy, gives us unexpected courage or prompts us to be compassionate, grateful or loving. Watching for these experiences and deepening the feelings might help to keep depression at bay.

# SOME TIPS FOR GOOD RELATIONSHIPS

I believe we have some of our greatest challenges and opportunities for growth within our closest relationships. This is because, not only are we dealing with these people most often, but we have our deepest feelings for them and invest a lot of energy in getting along with them. Although they are friends, lovers, and family, they can still be very different from us in background and experience. It helps if we remember that we were all born innocent and harmless, but have each been moulded by our life circumstances and those around us until we've ended up as we are today with our hurts and emotions often unacknowledged inside us. These cause us to react a certain way. We have no way of really knowing how another feels or what makes them behave as they do. We often don't even know why *we* react as we do to certain stimuli (why some people or happenings 'push our buttons' in a negative way).

In my search for ways to remain calm and peaceful, I have had to think a lot about relating, especially to those I love, and I'm sure I still have more to learn. I have also noticed how often the subject of relationships crops up in conversations with others as a cause for some challenges. What I have found helpful as one of the key factors is to remember the word **love**. Because I love someone, I don't want to be at war with them even if I do disagree with their words or actions, and I do want to be a helpful and pleasant companion, if possible. I also believe that **respect** is another important word to keep in mind, especially when dealing with different beliefs, opinions, or ways of doing things. We can all have a tendency to think our way is the right way, but it's only really right for us, not necessarily for any other human being. **Accepting** everyone's differences makes life so much less aggravating and more relaxing, because we're not then trying to change anyone's point of view (still less their behaviour or personality). An attitude of **tolerance** goes a long way in creating harmonious dealings with others.

I'm not saying that we should meekly go along with everybody's way of being when it affects our life. Non-violent communication with another about what we find difficult or how we are feeling about something is often very necessary, and talking things over is essential for any close relationship to work harmoniously, as long as both parties get an equal hearing. Especially in a new romantic relationship, it's vital to discover each other's views on certain important topics if we are to get on happily in the longer term. It's so easy to be blinded by the excitement and freshness of it all and not notice the areas where there are big incompatibilities that are difficult to resolve later.

Well, making relationships work is a subject copiously covered by books, workshops, therapists and on the internet. I am only scratching the surface here with some things I have found to help me that you might like to try for yourself.

1. Rather than belittling or criticizing, honour the other's behaviour and preferences that are different from yours, such as being quiet in the morning; not jumping up to clear up immediately after meals; going to bed early; not drinking alcohol.
2. Don't mock failings or challenges, such as being forgetful or unfit.
3. Don't try to change the way the other does something unless there's a very good reason. Your own way might appear better to you, but does that really matter? E.g., putting away shopping; preparing a meal; driving.
4. Be gentle when offering help, advice, or reminders. It's probably best to ask first whether your advice or opinion is wanted, or give a good reason for offering it, such as a safety issue or if they appear to have forgotten something important. When offering advice, do it gently or in the form of a question, such as "Is it a good idea to..."
5. Don't second guess what the other feels or what he or she is thinking. If necessary, ask.
6. Remember that others come from different backgrounds and experience, and their truth is right for them just as yours is right for you. e.g. duties to parents; spending priorities.
7. Stick up for what is right for you as long as it doesn't harm or adversely affect the other, e.g. having a rest during the day; not eating meat; showering every day; meditating.
8. When a negative thought about the other occurs (a judgement), make yourself appreciate something good about them instead.

9. Be patient so that you can stay calm and peaceful inside.
10. Start every day afresh, resolving not to repeat the same mistakes.
11. Don't take too much interest in what the other is doing if it doesn't directly involve you, unless invited to or to be supportive. Concentrate on your own activities.
12. When in disagreement, ask yourself which is more important: to be right or to have a harmonious relationship? If necessary, agree to differ.
13. Try not to leave an argument open, i.e., don't walk out in a temper; don't go to bed without making up.
14. Don't assume their anger/sadness/frustration is your fault. Allow for the other being stressed by something else.
15. Be honest about how you feel and don't be afraid to say "No" to anything that doesn't feel right for you.
16. If feeling irritated by the other's behaviour, try to focus more on your own activity or walk away and take some deep breaths before saying anything. Change your own *reaction* rather than trying to change their actions. It is well known that others' behaviours that 'push our buttons' can often be traits we exhibit ourselves (the mirroring principle). This might be worth considering from a self-development point of view.
17. When disagreeing, keep to the matter in hand without referring back to previous happenings.
18. If you feel angry about a friend or family member, counteract it with gratitude for having them in your life.
19. If someone criticises you, try not to react defensively. Be prepared to look at their comment (then or later)

to see if it might be justified. If you decide it's not, rather than taking it personally, see it as their ego needing a boost or an emotion they have that needs an outlet, e.g. jealousy, frustration, fear, insecurity, and let it go.

20. We all have different ways of showing our love and of feeling loved, and this is worth bearing in mind and possibly discussing with those closest to you. For example, some people feel loved by a show of physical affection while others prefer to be verbally praised or appreciated. Yet others look for offers of help as proof that they are loved, or for gifts. Then there are those who love and feel loved through intimate conversation or shared interests. There are three factors that enhance any relationship, and these are worth keeping in mind—acceptance, respect, and love. Try not to lose sight of any of these, if you want a relationship to be fair and successful.
21. It can be easy to take for granted those who are closest to us and, although we really love them, we may behave as if we don't when other things are on our mind. Staying aware should enable us to correct this behaviour, and it can be a good 'trick' to ask yourself whether you would treat a new friend or potential lover in such a way, and whether you are being respectful. We are usually on our best behaviour in such circumstances, so why not show yourself in this best light for those who really matter?

This is, of course, far from an exhaustive list and doesn't feel like a subject that needs any special exercises, as we are exercising our ability to relate harmoniously most of the time with everyone around us, not only those we dearly love but work colleagues, school friends, best friends, relatives, and all those we have to deal with in everyday life. I do suggest, though, that you occasionally re-read the list as a reminder and, if you find yourself having difficulties in a particular relationship, aim to recognise which tip might apply and give it a try.

# FORGIVENESS VIA UNDERSTANDING

Bearing in mind that our aim here is to reduce our stress and enable ourselves to feel calm and peaceful more of the time (and hence help our bodies to stay healthy), we must look at our negative and possibly difficult reactions to what we consider as people doing wrong. There will be times when the urge to judge someone as bad or evil for their actions is very hard to resist, especially when those actions touch on our own life. It may be an emotional or physical attack on ourselves, someone we love or care about, our way of life and freedoms, or even something we hear about in the media when someone's action causes suffering to others. We label these actions and/or the people as unforgivable.

Many of the inspirational, spiritual and self-development writings that I've come across advocate forgiveness as an important ability to develop. There are examples in history, and sometimes in the present day, when we hear of those who achieve this aim and harbour no negative feelings towards others, even when personally harmed.

In discussing this topic with others, I've noticed that it can bring out strong emotions, both for and against forgiving, so I feel it needs consideration here. It is a subject that is hugely coloured by personal beliefs and background, and the degree of suffering experienced, both currently and previously, but please bear with me while I offer some ideas.

Let's begin by peeling back to basics and look at how unforgiveness affects each of us as an individual. Here's a little exercise to try, which shouldn't go deep enough or last long enough to cause any lasting harm.

**Exercise 1:**

1. **Bring to mind someone you think would be hard for you to forgive. If you are fortunate enough to have no personal situations to relate this to, consider someone or a group or corporation on the world stage whose actions you see as harmful or cruel.**
2. **Think about what they do or did that you consider is unforgivable, and concentrate on that for a few moments.**
3. **Now notice how you are feeling emotionally and where your body is reacting. Are you gritting your teeth, clenching your fists? Are you feeling sensations of contracting muscles, maybe in your face or stomach or shoulders? Do you feel angry,**

**vicious, vindictive, revengeful, or ready for a fight, or is there a chronic hate or resentment festering away inside?**

4. **Once you've taken note of all these feelings, take your mind off the subject, have a few deep, long breaths, smile, and think of a 'smiley' or two. It was just an exercise to help your understanding, and we don't want all those feelings to stay around.**

So, I hope this exercise has shown you the effect that this very negative judgement has on the peace of your mind and body, and that, if you were harbouring these feelings long-term, you would be prolonging that effect. When you are doing all this to yourself and causing all this stress, is the other party feeling any harm, stress, or punishment? No, they are probably unaware of it all, so you are only punishing yourself!And, furthermore, if you forgive them once and for all, whose body relaxes, loses a lot of negative emotions and background bitterness? Yours of course.

OK, I know from personal experience that it's not that easy. It takes more than just realising the self-preservation value of forgiveness and depends very much on the situation in question, but I ask that you consider the following in relation to this subject.

First of all, forgiving does not mean or need condoning the action. We have to judge what people do in order to decide on our own moral values and ethics. We do this best by what feels right in our heart or our gut, rather than following the views and opinions of others. This gives us a personal set of standards for our own actions.

Of course, it's natural to sometimes feel negative emotions; they are part of our make-up, and certain circumstances will bring about anger, resentment, hatred of varying intensity. What we need to avoid is letting them hang around or keep coming back, affecting our peace and calm. So, when these feelings arise over the behaviour of someone, before we even try to find forgiveness for them, we need to vent the feelings. Depending on the situation, it might be appropriate to let the other person hear or see how you feel, if this is not going to cause further harm by escalating and prolonging the conflict. If this option would cause an escalation of the situation, I would recommend venting your feelings in private, using some physical action, if possible, to disperse the adrenalin and loosen the body tensions that have arisen. Actions such as yelling, foot stamping, punching a pillow, going for a run can all help. I have even found that writing down all my angry thoughts can be very helpful.

My next step would be to make understanding my goal. In fact, in some ways I consider this as good as forgiving. In order to need to forgive, I have had to judge someone as bad, and I don't always feel qualified or entitled to make that judgement, having no doubt caused some hurt{s} somewhere along my own life for which I would surely want to be understood.

In any situation that causes strife between parties, each brings to that event the conditioning and the result of all the good and bad experiences their life has brought them. We all are also made of different genes and have differing dispositions as a result of all this. There are bound to be clashes of personality, beliefs, ethics, and reactions at times. How can we know why someone behaves a certain way without having lived their life, or feeling how they feel as a result of their experiences?

We all have 'baggage' (past hurts and the resulting unhelpful aspects of our personality)—some more than others—and may exhibit behaviours that others see as bad or are actually harmful. If the injured party can remind themselves of how different we all are, because of our backgrounds, hardships, upbringing, beliefs, etc., they might be able to make some allowance for the offending behaviour, considering that anyone might exhibit that behaviour in the same shoes.

Having reached this far in the process, it then comes down to acceptance. In fact, if we find the effort to understand too difficult, we might have to settle for acceptance instead, remembering that we are striving to move away from stress and into calm. As long as we are harbouring those difficult and negative thoughts and feelings towards someone, we will be stressed whenever they get triggered again.

Sadly, within our human race there are some beings who are so damaged that they have lost all sense of moral integrity, have no feelings of empathy or belonging, and see all others as enemies or irrelevant beings. Therefore, they have no qualms about causing harm to others. It might even be that they are mentally sick. This results in actions that are labelled as 'wrong 'or 'evil', whatever the background of the perpetrator might be. In such cases, we may find forgiveness beyond us, but we still need to avoid dwelling on our bitter or resentful thoughts for the sake of our own well-being. In such a case, we might have to accept that we were wronged and may never understand why this happened or be able to forgive. The important thing then is to decide to move on, letting go of those negative thoughts, rather than harbouring vengeful feelings or developing a victim mentality.

I'd like to say that it really comes down to love for everyone at a soul level, but in the early stages of getting to know ourselves and watching what causes our good and bad emotions, this concept can be just too big a leap. We may eventually be able to see that it is those certain actions that are wrong, bad, or evil, rather than the perpetrators themselves.

## GUILT, SHAME AND SELF-FORGIVENESS

If you think back to those preventer categories of places that your mind wanders off to, sometimes causing you stress, one of the distractions taking you away from the present moment is 'me'. This may be finding yourself worrying about what others think of you, whether they like, love or care about you, whether you are 'good enough' for them not to leave you. You might be comparing yourself with others, or wondering whether you are popular enough and have enough friends. It could be your physical appearance that preys on your mind. Whatever the case, you have to decide whether to stay with that worry or come back to your calm centre and whatever you are experiencing in the moment.

Something that can cause a lot of us stress, momentarily or for the long term, is the feeling of guilt. It might be regretting something we've said or done, and wishing we could withdraw it or turn back time to avoid it. It could be an old action from earlier in life that keeps coming back to upset us, or lingers permanently in the background, possibly making us feel unworthy. We may think, or have been told, that we are flawed, sinful, bad or some other derogatory terms, all of which affect and lower our self-esteem, and steal our peace of mind.

Some people will counteract these feelings by creating stories to justify their actions and/or blame others, but this can be ineffective as they cannot fool themselves and, if they look deeply within, they will find that the shame still remains there. Alternatively, guilt can cause a person to develop a righteous, superior attitude to counteract the difficult emotions and fears that the guilt and shame thoughts have created.

So, what could we do to overcome these emotions that are stealing our peace and calm? I believe that, as with any thoughts or feelings that we find are causing us disturbance, we have to give some time and effort to face and feel them, and dig down inside us to discover their origin. There is no telling how long this might take, as it could be achieved in one focused session or take frequent efforts, depending how ingrained the feelings are and how deep you need to go. You might manage it alone or need the support of a friend or counsellor. We all have different ways of doing this sort of work, and you will know what suits you best, but all methods require us, first, to go inside to notice and feel the emotions. Sometimes just noticing, feeling and realising the futility of those thoughts can be enough to release us from the stress.

Of course, the ultimate goal is to be free of the stress these feelings bring or the unhelpful behaviours they might be causing, and this requires understanding and hence forgiveness. We must be able to forgive ourselves if we are to forgive others. It might be that, finding past experiences where you've been shamed or accused of being guilty by others, you are able to see where the origins are, and by understanding the dynamics of that event you can see how they still get triggered. As a child, you may have been reprimanded for something that upset an adult or you may have felt responsible for another's upset, even if you can't see how you caused it.

The way I have dealt with guilt from childhood was to remind myself that I knew no better at the time, and that I am no longer that same person, having matured, grown, and learnt better ways to behave. What we may consider 'sins' from later in life might be forgiven by understanding what conditions at the time caused the behaviour. We can then admit our mistake or carelessness and feel remorse for any harm we caused. It might help, in some cases, to make amends, if possible, without condoning the words or actions that we regret. The thing then is to put the incident to rest.

It's important to remember, yet again, that we are all so different. Someone might be upset by my action or words, despite me having the best of intentions. Most of the time, we have no idea why another person behaves the way they do. Even someone we meet briefly, such as a shop assistant, might react negatively to something we do or say, and this could be because of something worrying or painful that is going on in their life. A helpful strategy is to presume this is the case and give the other the benefit of the doubt, which, in itself, is a form of forgiveness. We cannot be held responsible for how the other reacts and, if we are made to feel otherwise in more important cases or with those close to us, some discussion is needed to achieve mutual understanding. When someone blames or accuses you, it isn't always your fault; how they feel is determined by their own issues. On the other hand, if you decide that you have been careless or unkind or that your actions are responsible for some hurt or harm, having made amends as best you can in words or actions, forgive yourself for the mistake and resolve to learn from it.

There is another cause of guilt that is milder but certainly worth working on. Do you ever feel like taking a break from chores and just chilling out, say in the evening or at the weekend, while you have a mental list of jobs that need doing? Does this lead you to try to relax while finding a voice in your head telling you that you 'should' be doing...? This has been one of my problems, having had a parent who always voiced the opinion that any time I spent reading, for instance, was a waste of time or even downright lazy. On similar lines is the guilt we can feel about needing to do things for others, or even just keeping in touch with them. It is inevitable that some of the people in our lives no longer share the same interests or beliefs. It feels as if we are no longer on the same 'waveband', but, out of habit or through a sense of duty, we feel obliged to stay in touch with them, and know that guilt would kick in again if we were to say "No".

We need a solution to prevent this scenario. One way out of this is to avoid ever using the word 'should'. 'Could 'makes a good substitute, as this leaves a space for choice and option. It's better not to do something than to do it with resentment or bad feeling. Another solution I have used is to look into where this type of guilt originates. In my illustration, this was from my mother, so, with awareness, I say to that voice within:"There are no shoulds or oughts, Mum. I'm living my life my way, thank you." The secret is to notice this guilt arising to disturb your peace, and then decide whether you want to follow the voice and carry out the duty or chore, or whether you want to carry on with your personal choice for that time.

**Exercise 2:**

1. **Make a list of activities you enjoy about which you sometimes feel guilty, such as enjoying a hobby or pastime, or just watching television.**
2. **Notice the words you say to yourself in these circumstances, and consider where they come from, e.g. do you hear a parent, teacher, partner saying them?**
3. **See if you can change any of the words used, such as 'should' to 'could', 'idle' to 'relaxing' or 'being'.**

* * *

**Exercise 3:**

**Create for yourself some affirmations related to exercise 2. Some examples might be:**

- **My life is balanced between doing and being.**
- **Relaxing is good for my mind, body, and spirit.**
- **I am the master of my life.**
- **I acknowledge and regret the mistakes I have made, but let them go and move on from here.**

* * *

**Exercise 4:**

**Once you have felt into the emotion and understood the circumstances, use your breath to let go of the guilt or shame you've been feeling:**

- **I breathe out guilt and breathe in forgiveness.**
- **I breathe out shame and breathe in freedom.**

# TWO TROUBLE-MAKERS—ATTACHMENT AND EXPECTATION

Among the preventers of our peace, we've already seen how fighting reality and fretting, or worrying about the past and future, can sabotage our efforts to stay calm and how we can cause ourselves stress by imagining scenarios about ourselves and others—taking us away from what is real and what is happening in the present moment for us to enjoy. Hopefully, we have learnt by now that, with awareness, we can watch unhelpful thoughts taking us over and creating emotions that we don't want, and we're getting better at being the masters of our minds rather than have them control us.

Most of our disturbing thoughts can be slotted into one of the preventer categories, but some are worthy of deeper consideration. Anyone who has looked into the teachings of the Buddha will recognise **attachment** and **expectation** as two states he recommended we avoid. A large portion of the world's population aim to live by the Buddha's teachings as he suggested many ways for us to avoid suffering, having discovered during his contemplations and meditations that we cause so much of our own suffering through our attitudes and reactions to our everyday circumstances. While learning to remain calm and peaceful doesn't necessitate studying Buddhism in any detail, I have to say that I have found some of the teachings very helpful, especially when related to everyday life by authors such as Jack Kornfield. This may or may not be a subject you wish to explore.

I am offering some thoughts and findings about these two subjects because I have noticed sometimes how my own discontent and even stress can be traced back to them. So, let's look at these two trouble-makers in case you find them stealing your calm as well.

## ATTACHMENT

This one can lead to fear of loss, and devastation in the case of loss, both harmful and unpleasant emotions for us to experience. We see them come into play at a very early age when toddlers begin to identify objects as belonging to them and resent having them removed. They often make their objection and anguish clear in no uncertain terms!As we grow up, we may make less noise about such occurrences, but the emotion might be just as powerful and just as apparent in our body. As usual, I am asking you to get into the feelings involved here in order to fully appreciate and understand the point, and we can use visualisation or imagination again.

**Exercise 1:**

**Looking around where you are now, if at home, or imagining being at home and looking around you, notice items that have a special meaning for you or that you are especially fond of that could not be replaced. The more special they are, the more attachment there will be for you. Then imagine how you would feel if you never saw the object or objects again. It might help if you imagine it actually being taken away by a stranger, or irreparably damaged or lost. Notice how you feel and stay with the feeling for a few moments. This will show you how attached you are, and you can repeat the exercise with other objects and notice the difference.**

Some lucky readers will have completed the exercise with no anguish. There may even be a minority who deliberately live with so few possessions that they experience no attachment problems about things. But what about attachment to people? I hear cries of protest that surely, we should be attached to those we love and devastated if we lose them, and far be it for me to say that we should not mourn the loss of loved ones as this is clearly a time when we need to acknowledge and fully feel our emotion in order to grow out of our despair. However, there can be a danger of letting our mourning lead us down into damaging negativity, or we might cling to the memory of the lost person to the extent that we are unable to move on in our own life. Furthermore, where people are concerned, we often cause our own suffering by worrying about losing someone when it might not even happen. It is attachment that causes this.

There can also be unhealthy attachments to people that keep us trapped in relationships that are not inspiring and uplifting for one or other party that we would be better to let go, such as with someone who is not available to us, or a controlling or incompatible partner with whom we feel secure (because we are used to them) but not happy. We might actually be attached to the safety rather than wanting to face the challenge of leaving, which would require courage and growth. This attachment starts as a natural, life-saving need in a baby or young child who could not survive without someone to meet their needs for nourishment and safety, but we can grow out of those needs once we can look after ourselves in the world. However, the inclination to get attached to people and things can persist if we let it, and especially if our basic needs were not met in childhood, or we have suffered a devastating loss in the past.

I have no wish for you to imagine losing anyone you love, but I hope that the next exercise will highlight for you some of the other ways in which we may become attached so that you can practise noticing when you are being affected by any such situations.

**Exercise 2:**

**Each letter has situations relating to something we can get attached to. Either imagine the examples given or think up your own and notice how attached you would be in each case. Some will have more impact than others and some will not affect you at all.**

| | |
|---|---|
| a) Status: | You get demoted at work and have a less impressive title.<br>You have to write 'divorced' on a form for the first time. |
| b) Money: | You lose your job and have no other form of income.<br>Your shares' value plummets. |
| c) Dwelling: | You involuntarily have to move into a much smaller dwelling.<br>You have to move to an area you really don't like. |
| d) Privacy: | You have to live with others after enjoying your own space for years.<br>You have to sleep in a dormitory with others. |
| e) Beliefs: | Beliefs you have had since childhood are challenged by new information. |
| f) Fitness: | Your life is disrupted by accident or illness.<br>You notice you can't run upstairs easily any more. |
| g) Freedom: | You have to become a full-time carer for a friend or family member.<br>You have to give up driving. |

h) Youth: You reach the next big birthday that you are dreading.
You claim your first age concession or bus pass as a pensioner.
You notice your first grey hairs.

i) Image: You think of yourself a certain way (kind/friendly/cheerful, etc.) and hear someone describe you as the opposite.

j) Role: You lose a role you've become used to such as parent, student, leader, carer, friend.

k) An outcome: A happy surprise you plan for someone disappoints them instead.
The holiday destination you chose isn't as good as it looked in the brochure.

I suppose you could say that you see no harm in being attached to some or all of these things (and the many others that are possible), but I hope that you can now see how they are pitfalls for feeling bad when the attachment is challenged. Whenever you notice that you are feeling fearful or insecure, it might be that something you are attached to is being threatened, and discovering what it is may help your understanding and acceptance. Because of its similarity, the last attachment on the list leads us nicely on to...

## EXPECTATIONS

I must admit to this being one of my main pitfalls, despite friends warning me that being an optimist can lead to disappointment. I still prefer to expect good outcomes, but now I realise that I mustn't get attached to that expectation. Having a lively imagination is also a stumbling block where expectation is concerned, and I sympathise with readers who have this similarity to me. Still, as usual, being aware of what we are doing to ourselves with our thoughts is the key to avoiding undue suffering when our expectations are not met and, better still, to catching and stopping ourselves when we find we're dreaming up the results that we want.

**Exercise 3:**

**It would be impossible to list all the expectations we might have, as each person is capable of so many every moment of the day. However, just to help you focus on the subject, here are a few examples for you to consider. Then I'd like you to list for yourself some examples from your own life of when something didn't turn out as you had hoped, and to remember the grief that caused you. By doing this, I have found that I've become more aware of when I am heading for another pitfall with my own expectations.**

**We might tend to expect:**

- **people to behave in a certain way (especially family and friends)**
- **praise, reward, or thanks for something we've done**
- **events we've planned to be enjoyable**

- **to always be healthy and fit**
- **summer to be sunny and warm**
- **a new job/car/home/partner to be better than the old one**
- **the above four, or more money to bring us more happiness**
- **the latest diet to improve our figure**
- **that our trying to achieve something is bound to fail (which can also be very damaging to our growth by preventing us taking on challenging and expanding ourselves).**

**And on and on in a never-ending list to watch out for!**

Hopes and dreams might be thought of as kinds of expectations. Do practising Buddhists have them? I don't know the answer to this, but I personally think that life would have less joy and fun without them. I think the trick is to keep them in mind in a vague and serene way, always remembering that, if they do come true, they might not turn out as we imagined them and, if they don't come to pass, they weren't meant to be.

There are many who believe we can manifest anything we want through our thoughts, and some who clearly do achieve great success at this. It entails expecting certain definite results, but the unswerving belief, trust and certainty needed for this practice can be hard to cultivate.

So, how do we deal with them when they arise, these two trouble-makers? Well, the important point to remember is that we always have a choice about what to think. We have to keep coming back to this fact and alter what we are thinking if it might lead us to suffering. As I said, I still prefer to be an optimist, but now I temper that with an acceptance that things and people are just as they are, which might not always fit my expectation. In fact, the most common expectation people have seems to be about other people. Our tendency is to expect everyone to be like us in their likes, dislikes, beliefs, preferences, and behaviours, but, hopefully, we have accepted by now that this isn't the case.

It might help to dig deep to find where our expectations originate, which could involve looking back at our life's experiences and conditioning. We're often expecting things and people to be a certain way simply because we were taught so by others passing on their opinions and beliefs to us. We may subconsciously expect certain outcomes—good or bad—because of experiences we've had in life. Once we are aware of their origins, these expectations should become less automatic.

Sometimes we will have to let go of people or things we'd rather keep near us, and our life circumstances are bound to change with time. Acceptance again comes to the rescue. It didn't happen for me overnight: I had to work at it and my mind has given me lots of opportunity for practice!I wish you luck with yours.

# THINGS ALONG THE WAY—2

## MINDFULNESS

We hear this word a lot lately. Buddhists have been used to it, as it's been part of Buddhist practice since that began about 2500 years ago. For all our thinking to the contrary, we are actually pretty slow learners here in the west, and now mindfulness books and courses abound as we wake up to a technique that can beat stress, help us prevent it in the first place and has been shown by researchers to improve our health and longevity through developing an inner peace.

I'm hoping that the claims I've just listed sound familiar, as they are exactly what we have been working on achieving so far in this guide So, how is mindfulness different from awareness then? Well, the differences are rather subtle but important, I think. It might just be my perception, but I feel that staying aware of what is going on inside and around us is easier to accomplish than what is advocated by mindfulness training. I tried for years to become more mindful and began to despair of ever achieving it, but then found that being aware enough to notice my thoughts, feelings and reactions was more do-able and, more importantly, enabled me to change any of those that were causing me to suffer.

Both practices require us to be in the present moment and to watch our thoughts. Then they differ as follows:

- **Mindfulness** asks us, during a particular activity, to let each irrelevant thought float away without giving it any attention, so that we stay present in and concentrate on the activity (even if that is just sitting and breathing).
- **Awareness** also keeps us in the present moment and involves noticing whether the thought is helpful to our well-being or not.
- Doing something **mindfully** means focusing all our attention on it in detail.
- Living with **awareness** helps us notice more of what is going on within and around us and the effect it all has on our feeling of well-being and inner peace. It also enables us to understand better ourselves and others.

For example, **mindfully walking** would mean slowly placing down each foot, noticing the feel of your feet on the ground, the muscles you are using, and which other parts of your body are involved. You would notice how your clothes feel on you and the air against your skin, as well as any smells or sounds around. You would immerse yourself totally in the experience, and the concentration would cause you to let go of any thoughts that might otherwise arise while you are walking.

Another example could be **mindfully eating**, and I got some friends to try this once, asking them to choose a nut, a piece of chocolate or a mandarin segment, and then to do the following exercise that you might like to try for yourself.

**Exercise 1:**

1. **Choose something small to eat, such as a piece of fruit or a nut.**
2. **First of all, study its texture and shape in your hand, and look at its shape and colour. Does it have a smell?**
3. **Put it in your mouth, but don't chew yet.**
4. **Feel how it tastes already and how big it feels. Is it cold, smooth, soft? Is it making your mouth water?**
5. **Now begin to chew it very slowly. Notice how you move it about in your mouth and how the taste and texture change. Concentrate on all of this until it is chewed up enough to swallow.**
6. **Continue to appreciate the taste as it passes down your throat and notice the aftertaste left in your mouth.**

In the discussion after the exercise, I learnt that my friends had all chosen the Brazil nut because they didn't trust they could eat the chocolate slowly, and also hoped they'd be 'rewarded' afterwards by being able to down the chocolate and fruit in their normal fashion!In a way, this confirmed to me how difficult and alien it is to most of us to live our lives in full mindfulness. Of course, this is taking the practice to the extreme, which is probably more than most of us want to achieve anyway. I do still allot myself mindful periods when I make a real effort to fully concentrate on every single thing I do, but I can't say that

I really enjoy it. It does keep me peaceful and I'm less forgetful in that frame of mind, so I can see that I might benefit from achieving it more often.

Despite it not suiting me, I do thoroughly recommend that you look into the topic on the internet or by reading one of the many books on the subject, such as the one in my book list which gives a full eight-week course and CD. In a way it's like a more intense version of what we are working on through these pages and you will find several overlaps in the methods. This could either serve to reinforce what you are learning here, or you might find that you enjoy the process and have no trouble at all in totally mastering its techniques. Mindfulness courses are also offered as a therapy and may be available where you live.

One thing that trying the mindfulness practice has taught me is the benefit of **slowing down**. As you will have noticed in the eating exercise, being mindful does result in doing things more slowly and carefully. This slowing down alone can allow more time for the awareness we are trying to achieve, prevent the build-up of stress and tension, and lead to fewer mistakes and forgetfulness. Amazingly, it doesn't seem to result in everything taking much longer, as the smooth efficiency that results from combining slowness and awareness often seems to enable me to achieve more in the long run. The other interesting effect that it has is to slow the mind so that thoughts aren't racing around, falling over each other and causing a general distraction from what I am supposed to be concentrating on. Why not try it now and then and see what it does for you?

**Exercise 2:**

**When you finish reading this section and start to get on with whatever activity you plan to do next, consciously make yourself move slowly enough to be mindful of the movements you are making and the actions you are carrying out. If you have to move from place to place, do it deliberately slowly and with ease, noticing any tensions in your body as you go. (No—watching television will not count for this exercise!)**

**When you feel you've practised enough, just stop for a short while to consider how you now feel and how it felt during the exercise.**

A little fun activity you might like to try is to do some mindful doodling or colouring. Again, some friends and I have done this exercise and found that it had some clear benefits. It was a relaxing way to spend a little time, doing something that we would not normally allow ourselves to do, classing it as a 'waste of time', and it somehow slowed the mind's activity for the period involved. Allowing yourself to 'waste time', if that is how you would normally consider it, is a constructive and effective way of breaking free from old conditioning.

**Exercise 3:**

1. **Set aside a period of not less than 30 minutes when you won't be interrupted.**
2. **Find yourself some plain paper or a colouring book and some colouring pens or pencils.**
3. **If you haven't a colouring book, start to draw randomly whatever comes (I call it 'taking a line for a walk'), or just start to doodle.**
4. **Once you have created some shapes, set about filling in the shapes with different colours or patterns, being totally absorbed in what you're doing.**

**Please note that, if you're doing the exercise with friends, you shouldn't be chatting because you have to focus on the task in hand. Also, try to ensure that you don't follow any 'rules' about the drawing or colouring, but let the inspiration come naturally.**

* * *

**Exercise 4:**

**During the next week or so, try to complete one activity per day as mindfully as you can. Things like washing up or getting dressed are good examples to try at first or, if you have chores to do, how about weeding or painting mindfully?**

# ATTITUDE—A CHOICE

Attitude isn't just something that challenging teenagers have. The word has become a derogatory term in recent years, but it is really something we all have all the time. It can apply to our general way of being or become a temporary state that we go into either automatically, because of past conditioning or by choice. When you come to think of it, we always have some attitude or other towards whatever is going on.

I expect we can all bring to mind people with general attitudes in the various categories such as serious, happy-go-lucky, miserable, arrogant, nervous, relaxed, positive, etc. because they exhibit these traits most of the time, and this attitude colours their whole perception of life and everything around them, as well as all activities they undertake. They may or may not be contented with how they feel. Most people would say that it's just how they are and they can't change it. Wrong!

Then there are the occasions when someone might say "I didn't like his attitude", "Her attitude wasn't at all helpful" or "Well, that's a good attitude to have towards it". On these occasions, the attitude may have been in response to something that triggered the person to react a certain way, or may have been consciously chosen for the situation. What I have discovered is that this ability to choose our attitude to circumstances is so useful, and, what's more, with enough practice, we can actually alter how we feel about life in general if we wish. In some ways, we have been working on our attitudes through these steps and are, hopefully, developing more positive, confident, relaxed ones to what life sends us.

In my view, a **positive** attitude is the most valuable as it enables us to deal with most circumstances. Being positive prevents us judging ourselves or others by making us look for the good traits. It helps us to see challenges as opportunities for growth, and gives us courage, by fostering belief in a positive outcome for our endeavours. Positive thinking boosts self-esteem and can encourage us out of our comfort zone to try things that may bring us more fulfilment. A positive attitude lifts the spirit, keeping us away from the dangers of depression, and can even help the body to heal. This has been documented in many books about people recovering from serious, life-threatening disease by developing a positive attitude towards their ability to cure themselves. There are also many accounts of a positive attitude helping people through terrible traumas and ordeals such as concentration camps, that could have crushed their spirit into giving up on life.

Another attitude that I feel is important to adopt is a relaxed one. Having a relaxed attitude can apply to so many aspects of life. I decided some time ago to make **relax** my word from now on, not so that I would spend time lounging about all day but in order to have that attitude towards what people think of me, how to spend my time, lists of chores to be done, other people's behaviour, getting older, my appearance, the future, saying what I believe, and many other things. It's also more comfortable to carry out chores and take part in activities in a relaxed way rather than in a race against time or with resistance.

An attitude of **gratitude** can do wonders for how we feel. As I've covered elsewhere, we can always find something to be grateful for and this attitude is the perfect antidote for self-pity, discontent, and many negative feelings.

A **tolerant** attitude is a great one for enabling us to accept reality rather than fighting it, and prevents us complaining about circumstances. It is particularly useful when having to deal with people whose behaviours or personalities we find difficult.

I hope you can see now how important attitude is to how we feel, so that, through the awareness that you are now exercising on a regular basis (I hope!), you begin to notice whether your current attitude to what's happening, or to life in general, is helpful or not. And, if not, you simply need to change it!

# LAST THING ALONG THE WAY—A LITTLE DEEPER IF YOU CHOOSE

## HUMAN SPIRIT AND THE GREAT MYSTERY

My intention with this heading is to make this section sound absolutely optional. It is not vital to you achieving happiness that you agree with my beliefs (at least I don't think so), but consideration of this subject has been a part of my personal growth as a result of reading such a variety of books.

I think it must be clear by now that the main theme of practice that I have advocated throughout is that of awareness. By staying aware as much as possible, we notice all the details of life as it happens around us, as well as our own responses to everything. We achieve this by operating from what I have been calling 'the real me'. So, who or what is this 'real me'?

I hope we can by now agree that it's not the personality self or ego who is a result of all that we've experienced up to this point in life. The real me is the part that watches the personality and remains calm and still, whatever happens. She seems to be that still, small voice who knows the best action to take. I can discover from her the wisest choice when decisions have to be made, and she's a part of me that is always in the present moment while my mind and ego are off in places that can make me suffer.

The real me may be known by many other names—higher self, conscience, intuition, spirit, soul, observer, light being, and many more. Some of the authors I have read consider that, within this part of each of us, we have all the answers we could ever need because it is here that we connect to a greater consciousness or universal mind.

It may be that the real me is the part that is connected in an energetic way with absolutely everything because it is a tiny part of one great whole. This is the one great whole who has many names, of which the most common are God and Allah. I personally can't think of creation being carried out by a personified being, although I see that this does work for a huge percentage of the human population. I realise that there is a life force within everything—more animated in some forms than others—but, because I feel that we have no concrete evidence about its origins, I prefer to call this creative intelligence the Great Mystery or Source. My preferred view is that everything is energy, and that energy may be what we call consciousness. Through natural laws this consciousness materialises the myriad forms from the tiniest cell to the biggest celestial body.

Along with this understanding, I have to believe that everything also has access to this creative power. Because humankind has evolved such imaginative power and such effective means of communication, we are proof of this creative ability within us.

How else can it be that we have invented so much—for good and bad—during our time on Earth?

So enough of my philosophising and back to the practicalities. The reason I offer this glimpse into my beliefs is that I feel I have proven for myself that I create my own reality to a great extent, especially my inner reality. I have spent time with people who have a basically negative attitude and I notice how differently we see the world, the people in it and the situations we find ourselves in. By focusing on all that they consider wrong or not to their liking, they lose the capacity to see and appreciate what could bring them joy, and they thus create unnecessary stress for themselves. I have found that, by keeping my thoughts peaceful, positive and with a big dose of gratitude as much as I can, by staying aware and living from the real me, I tend to notice more of the good things in life and people, and can appreciate the beauty around us.

# SOME FAVOURITE METAPHORS

I find metaphors helpful, and others have reported that they help to remind them of some of their own shortcomings and how they can make better choices. Here are a few that come to mind that you might like to consider.

## LIFE'S A JIGSAW

We each have our own vital place in life, without which the big picture is incomplete. Each piece is unique and has an equally important part to play, as I suggested in the earlier section.

## DON'T SPOIL A NICE DINNER

You wouldn't want to spoil a good meal by pouring something distasteful all over it, would you? There is beauty all around and tranquillity within, but we miss both of these if we concentrate on what we don't want or don't have. When we fight reality or dwell in negativity, we are denying ourselves the chance to enjoy what is right in front of us in this moment, and prevent ourselves feeling calm and peaceful.

## WHY RUMMAGE THROUGH THE RUBBISH BIN?

Once we throw away our rubbish each day, we tend to forget it rather than keep sorting through it to see what's there, so why keep looking back at what has gone before, especially if it wasn't helpful? I know we have done some exercises involving the past but, once completed and used, these memories and their effect on us can be put away for collection and disposal, i.e. forgotten.

## AM I LOOKING IN A MIRROR?

Could it be that the fault I am seeing in this other person is something that I don't like in myself? Are they showing me something I could benefit from working on or changing? Mirror work is a useful psychological tool for discovering aspects of ourselves that are not helpful every time someone 'presses our buttons'.

## LOCKED IN A BOX?

How would you feel if you were threatened with the possibility of being locked inside a box for evermore? If we make no effort to change our unhelpful ways, live in past memories and stick rigidly to old beliefs without opening to new ideas or trying new experiences, we might as well be in a box—it may be a memory box—but it's still a box. Every new moment we live can be full of interest and the possibility to be expanded into and enjoyed.

## WHY EAT A POISON SANDWICH?

Tuna makes me as sick as a dog for some reason, so, when I find myself thinking something that clearly is making me suffer, I ask myself why I am eating a tuna sandwich. Remember that we can always choose what we think, and watch for our own self-sabotaging 'poison'.

## I TRUST MY MEAL IS COMING

I use affirmations sometimes to state what I would like to create in my life. I know I haven't covered manifestation in detail, but we did look at affirmations as a tool for creating more helpful beliefs and I might use something like "I am a confident public speaker". I know I need to repeat this often to bring about my desired result, but there is a danger of becoming despondent if I notice no improvement at first. I liken this lack of trust in a process to placing an order in a restaurant and not really believing that my meal will arrive. Do you usually keep checking with the waiter that your dinner is coming? I certainly don't. We need to trust the process.

## SOFT-CENTRED SWEET

One way that people find helpful for 'checking-in' is to imagine themselves coming into their soft centre, rather like a soft-centred sweet. The personality self/ego that has to deal with everything going on in my life and the people I meet is like the harder, outer part of the sweet, but there's a soft part, in the centre of my body, into which I can settle and feel relaxed and comfortable. Visualising this softness creates the feeling of calm peacefulness.

## THE OCTOPUS

When I become aware of my mind scattering off in all directions—other people, the future, fantasy, job lists, worries, etc.—I see it as an octopus with many tentacles. Then I choose to pull those tentacles back into my centre, making a feeling of wholeness as well as calming all the agitation.

## THE POT OF PAINT

I first thought of this one as a way of explaining to friends why I believe we should bless people that we call our enemies and those that do harm in a family or society, and I have referred to this elsewhere in the handbook. If we imagine the human race as a big pot of grey paint, it can either be lightened up by adding white pigment or made darker by adding black. If we then think of what we consider as wrong/bad/evil/negative as being caused by the black paint and we add our own negative feelings of hate/anger/revenge, we are making the pot still darker, rather than lightening it up or rebalancing it with the white paint of positive thoughts of love, kindness, compassion and forgiveness.

# BEFORE YOU GO—
# A FEW MORE STEPS TO JOY

We have to draw to a close at some point and I feel you should now have enough steps to bring you to increased inner peace. I must remind you that it has taken me years to sift these steps from all the teachings and practices I've come across, and that it is only by applying the techniques on a daily basis that I feel I have achieved the serenity I was seeking. As I wish you success on your journey, I list here a few more suggestions towards achieving a calm, peaceful and joyful life. Some of them are reminders of topics already covered that I feel are worth repeating, while others are in addition to the practices that I have been sharing with you so far, but which don't particularly fit into any of the sections of the handbook. It might be an idea to mark or make a note of a few that you feel you would like to add to your practice for a while, rather than trying to take in and remember them all at once. I appreciate that, after a major trauma or loss, being able to feel joy again may seem a long way off, but trying just a few of the following list may enable you to have glimpses of how joy can return, and encourage you to take a few steps in that direction.

1. On waking, give appreciation for three things in your life, even if only your safe night's sleep and your bed.
2. Choose one thing that you are going to do that day simply because you want to rather than have to, even if only a walk down the garden to smell the fresh air and look at a flower.
3. On rising, smile at yourself in the mirror and wish yourself, genuinely, a happy, joyful day.
4. Remember that it isn't what you do that brings you joy or not; it's how you feel about it. If you can't do what you most enjoy at the moment, decide to enjoy what you *are* doing.
5. Whenever you get the chance, hold open a door for someone, smile at someone or give a compliment. Being good to others helps us feel good about ourselves. Remember that smiling and being kind release chemicals that make us feel good.
6. Save jokes that you enjoy and notes about funny things that happen, and read them again if you feel low.
7. Sometimes allow yourself to sit and listen to a favourite song or piece of music, without doing anything else.
8. If you enjoy such activities, sing and/or dance sometimes, preferably every day.
9. Do some exercise, however little, to include some deep breathing into the belly. Try to keep smiling as you do it, and be grateful to your body for all its abilities and service to you.
10. Always be on the lookout for opportunities for fun and play, or see the funny side of life.

11. Acting the way you want to feel can help lead you to feeling that way.
12. Keep a notebook for recording happy events and gratitudes, however small.
13. Create a 'strokes and hugs' book of compliments, appreciations and kind things people say to you, and read it when your self-esteem is low.
14. Remember that happiness is a choice we make from within.
15. Watch for balance in your life. For example, between doing and being, work and play, company and solitude, mind, body, spirit, care for others, but also for yourself. Moderation is a good word to keep in mind in all things.
16. Be kind and forgiving to yourself, especially when feeling low or you think you've made a mistake.
17. Remember you are not your thoughts.
18. When struggling with a situation, decision or a difficult emotional reaction, check whether your ego is taking you over and, if so, aim to get back to your real, wiser self.
19. Remember to frequently check for and release body tension, especially where you most often hold it, such as shoulders, face, hands.
20. Break down big and challenging projects into small steps and feel satisfaction as you complete each one.
21. Avoid giving yourself unnecessary stress by taking on more than you can manage comfortably.
22. Write down lists rather than keeping chores and worries in your head.
23. Allow yourself to put things off sometimes and return to them when you feel like it.

24. When others are reacting stressfully, hold a calm space for them.
25. Be the change you want to see in the world. A peaceful world begins within each one of us.
26. Sometimes stop to ask yourself how you are feeling in this moment. Could you do with feeling better? What do you need to do to achieve this?

Even remembering some of the techniques can provide little islands of tranquillity in the midst of whatever storminess is going on within and around us.

So, now we part company, dear reader, with my sincere hope that these steps are, and will continue to be, leading you into that space of inner peace that is within each of us. The aim is, with practice, to remain there for longer and longer periods until it becomes a permanent state of being. I am aware of the temptation now to put this work aside and look for the next book or teacher, but I hope you will revisit or even re-read the material from time to time because, as we change and grow, so do the things that work for us. I have personally found that some of the practices work for me better now than they did originally. Our growth just never stops and I freely admit to still being a work in progress!

If any of this work has brought up difficult issues that you've found too hard to tackle on your own, I urge you to seek professional help. There is no shame in admitting that we have difficulties too big to face alone, and the right help can enable us to discover and deal with whatever is preventing us enjoying the calm and peaceful life we deserve.

By learning to live in a state of conscious awareness, and with the tools to enable us to deal with uncomfortable and unhelpful emotions as they arise, we should be able to live in a space where we can cope with most of what life sends us, and benefit from all the love, beauty, and joy we could wish for.

# MEET MY HELPERS—SOME BOOKS ALONG MY PATH (IN NO PARTICULAR ORDER)

**Some of these books refer to God. Let the name stand for whatever you believe is the intelligence/life force/consciousness that is behind creation and of which we are all a part.**

## WHY KINDNESS IS GOOD FOR YOU—David Hamilton

An explanation of the science behind oxytocin—the chemical connected with kindness—and how to make use of it. David shows how we can produce more of the chemical within our bodies and become kinder people. Some practical exercises too.

## HANDBOOK TO HIGHER CONSCIOUSNESS—Ken Keyes Jr

A workbook for overcoming our negative traits and converting addictions to preferences. It works through the seven energy centres of the body (chakras), dealing with issues related to each.

## A COURSE IN MIRACLES—Helen Schucman & William Thetford

A programme with a spiritual basis, emphasising forgiveness of self and others, and moving from fear to love.

## WIRED FOR JOY—Lauren Mellin

Explains how parts of the brain work and how we can 'rewire' ourselves with detailed practical techniques for moving out of stress towards a joyful state.

## MOLECULES OF EMOTION—Candace Pert

The science behind emotions by a scientist who has devoted her career to discovering the relationship between emotions and the chemicals and hormones of the body.

## MINDFULNESS—Mark Williams & Danny Penman

The eight- week course on how to be more mindful in meditation and everyday life, with projects to complete for each week.

## THE POWER OF NOW—Eckhart Tolle

Why we should live in the present moment and from our real selves (our presence).

## A NEW EARTH—Eckhart Tolle

Being present in the now and noticing what removes us from it. The ego and pain body's impact on our life and how to deal with them skilfully.

## THE ENDORPHIN EFFECT—William Bloom

The science of emotions and importance of the relationship between thoughts, emotions, and the body. Creating a strawberry list ('smileys') and additional exercises.

## QUIET YOUR MIND—John Selby

As the title says, John gives exercises and encouragement to deal with thoughts and their emotions.

## THE DIVINE MATRIX—Gregg Braden

Quantum physicist and geologist introduces his belief in a connected and creative universe of which each of us is a holographic part. The book also covers manifesting and has many strategies for positive living.

## PURE—Barefoot Doctor

Mental and physical exercises, including the use of visualisation and affirmations.

## THE WISE HEART—Jack Kornfield

Buddhist belief, psychology, and practice, with a lot of useful exercises and meditations. Many insights into how we cause our own suffering, and techniques to avoid doing so.

## YOU ASK AND IT IS GIVEN—Jerry & Esther Hicks

Exercises for improving mood and becoming more positive.

## YOU CAN HEAL YOUR LIFE—Louise Hay

Relating emotions to physical ailments and a good starter book for self-knowledge.

## THE GENTLE ART OF BLESSING—Pierre Pradavand

How to counteract negative and judgemental thoughts and beliefs by blessing everyone, with anecdotes of the efficacy of this technique.

## THE INVITATION; THE CALL; THE DANCE—Oriah Mountain Dreamer

Three books, based on Oriah's poems, using her life experiences and struggles to give helpful insights and advice for living everyday life to the full, from our spiritual selves, with encouragement to find our life's purpose through self-exploration. Many meditations included on specific subjects.

## PASSIONATE PRESENCE—Catherine Ingram

More encouragement to stay aware in all aspects of life.

## OPENING OUR HEARTS TO MEN—Susan Jeffers

Good advice for noticing how we relate in more ways than the title suggests, although focusing on women's attitudes to men and how to heal the unhelpful ones.

## THE BIOLOGY OF BELIEF—Bruce Lipton, PhD

A scientific explanation of cells, DNA, genes, and their part in our make-up; how the environment affects them and hence our physiology. The impact of the energies around and within us, including the energy of our thoughts.

## THE GIFT OF CHANGE; A RETURN TO LOVE—Marianne Williamson

In both books, Marianne refers to "A Course in Miracles" and discusses how to change our thoughts with an emphasis on the power of love, kindness, forgiveness, tolerance and being aware of the ego in self and others.

## LOVING WHAT IS—Byron Katie

A particular method of enquiry for when we are fighting reality, with examples.

## YOUR BODY SPEAKS YOUR MIND—Debbie Shapiro

Recognising what the body is telling us through its physical problems.

## BIO-SPIRITUALITY—P. A. Campbell & E. M. McMahon

A technique for dealing with emotions by staying with them and finding them in the body.

## THE PLACES THAT SCARE YOU—Pema Chodron

Descriptions of some of the Buddhist teachings and how they apply to everyday life, with exercises for the reader to practise and to use for self-discovery.

## INSPIRATION—Wayne Dyer

Encouragement for the spiritual journey, emphasising the need for positivity and lightness of attitude, with some suggested practices. Wayne Dyer has written over 40 books to encourage and help readers fulfil their potential and lead self-actualised lives.

## CHANGE YOUR THOUGHTS AND CHANGE YOUR LIFE—Wayne Dyer

A personal interpretation of the ancient wisdom of the Tao Te Ching, relating it to everyday modern life and how we can use it to create more peace and calm.

## REINVENTING THE BODY, RESURRECTING THE SOUL—Deepak Chopra

Awareness and the ability to change what's not helping us. Has exercises and reminder lists. A medical doctor and spiritual teacher, Deepak offers a lot of wisdom about our mind, body and spirit connection.

## YOU DO KNOW—Becky Walsh

Living from intuition rather than ego, with lots of ideas for dealing with everyday life and challenges; finding our purpose and being the best we can be.

## THE AWAKENED BRAIN—Lisa Miller

Scientific data on our neurological "wiring" for spirituality, and how to make use of it to beat depression.

These are just a tiny few of the many, many books that have helped me, and that I have loved reading. The bookshops and internet are brimming with self-help and spiritual growth books, and, of course, we now have podcasts, talks and blogs by so many wonderful teachers who want to pass on what they find helps them navigate their lives and bring them joy. I urge you to explore more deeply the topics that have felt most relevant to you through this work, as we never stop growing and developing more of our potential.

# WITH DEEP GRATITUDE

To all those sharing my journey through life, for their support and challenges along the way, and to the mysterious and creative Force that gives us life, and of which I believe we are all a part.

Printed in Great Britain
by Amazon